AFRICAN WRITERS SERIES
Editorial Adviser · Chinua Achebe

28

SHORT EAST AFRICAN PLAYS
IN ENGLISH

AFRICAN WRITERS SERIES

SHORT EAST AFRICAN PLAYS IN ENGLISH

Ten Plays in English
collected and introduced by

DAVID COOK and MILES LEE

HEINEMANN EDUCATIONAL BOOKS
LONDON NAIROBI IBADAN

Heinemann Educational Books Ltd
48 Charles Street, London W1X 8AH
POB 25080, Nairobi · PMB 5205, Ibadan
EDINBURGH HONG KONG SINGAPORE
MELBOURNE TORONTO AUCKLAND

ISBN 0 435 90028 5

© Heinemann Educational Books Ltd 1968
© Introduction and Notes David Cook and Miles Lee 1968
First published 1968
First published in the African Writers Series 1970

Printed in Malta by St Paul's Press

Contents

Introduction

In most East African communities dance has long been the main outlet for creative self-expression. Though in many places, with the spread of urbanization, the traditional dance-forms signifying birth, initiation, war, worship and death have lost their earlier key position in the life of village societies, yet dance-halls and night-clubs still allow town-dwellers to express their happiness, or overcome their worry and the effects of their labours in the city, through the medium of movement. Dance, music and song, all aspects of man's creative instincts, are as rhythmically powerful today in tarmaced Africa as in the more rural areas. And likewise the epic art of the narrator has survived by adapting itself to new conditions. The story-teller has become more of an actor than he used to be, and he now often enlists the help of his wife and friends to act out the tale he is telling; while he himself emphasizes the main thread of the narrative, his small supporting company embellishes the events with song and music and further words. So a link is formed between the arts of traditional dance and narration, and that of formal drama: and as different modes intermingle, new patterns emerge.

East Africans have been writing down play scripts in English for a good many years now. There are objections that can be raised against this practice. Drama is a fluent expression of the performer's whole being, and there is no doubt that the majority of people can interpret emotion more fully and freely in their mother tongue than they can in a second or foreign language. Furthermore, it may be said that scripted drama is an alien form which should not be allowed to overshadow performances growing more directly from East African tradition. However, experiments with travelling theatres have no more than confirmed what has been discovered in many widely separated places, that language is not an insuperable barrier to popular communication; and in lands with widely divergent vernaculars, drama which is to be more than local in its cast or audience must make bold, arbitrary decisions about the language employed and then set about to overcome the inevitable problems that are raised. On the second point, the editors of this book agree with most of the young writers we know, that Africa wants, needs, and can absorb every possible kind of play-acting; and the encouragement of one form is more likely to stimulate other forms than to create an artistic monopoly. Since drama is a vital, immediate human expression, East African groups, both in schools and elsewhere, inevitably call for a high proportion of plays rooted in their own part of the world. It is with the practical purpose in mind of increasing the number of suitable plays widely available that we have made this collection.

Our first thoughts have not therefore been literary. The relatively small body of African writing in English to date has easily fallen under the spotlight of reviewers. Kinds of writing that pour from British presses without being subjected to solemn criticism may well be the subject of elegant book reviews if the author happens to be African. This has sometimes made publishers hesitate to print unpretentious pieces for fear of rough handling by the critics, and on other occasions may have prompted them to argue the claims of minor works at inappropriate levels in self-defence. So we are pleased that the very mixed bag in this book has been allowed to steer its way into print between these extremes. We certainly believe that several of these short plays are good drama in every sense of the word. Those who have worked with amateur groups or in school in U.K. will know how difficult it is to find one-acters of this calibre even amidst the welter of material available there. Other items in this volume claim no other graces of language than those which serve to make them work effectively on a stage before a responsive audience. That has been our minimum entrance requirement, so to speak. As this is written, only one of these plays awaits its first performance, but this is already in rehearsal. Most of them have been successfully broadcast by Radio Uganda and other East African stations, and one by the African Service of the B.B.C. Perhaps one or two of them may be even more effective on the air than on the stage; but for the most part they move easily from one medium to the other. Seven were performed far and wide in Kenya and Uganda by the Makerere Travelling Theatre.

The two shortest pieces, *The Famine* and *The Mirror*, are in fact translations from the vernacular (Luganda and Runyoro/Rutoro) and are included here mainly as working demonstrations of what can easily be done in any language by someone who wants to create drama from local fables, stories and traditions. Joseph Mukasa-Balikuddembe worked these playlets up specially for the Travelling Theatre; he took each of the leading parts himself, and would ad lib at will from the basic script, adapting various allusions to whatever town we happened to be in, rather after the manner of the Commedia dell'Arte in Renaissance Italy. *Bones* also had a place in the Travelling Theatre, but in Swahili as *Mifupa*. This sketch was elaborated by the author in the role of the butcher with burlesque comic miming in keeping with the broad satirical idea—unfailingly a tumultuous success which unmistakably got home its points. *Third Party Insurance* is slight enough on paper, but can rattle along on the stage to keep an audience laughing at the farcical treatment of a simple, timeless theme.

The Trick stands on its own. Erisa Kironde has taken Synge's *Shadow of the Glen* and transplanted it, lock, stock and barrel into Uganda, so that it appears to have grown here. It is not easy to make this kind of adaptation without falling into mere wooden translation or losing entirely the spirit of the original. Erisa Kironde's success points to a fruitful field for extending East African drama, both in English and the vernaculars.

The other five serious plays form the main body of the book. Only one comment seems appropriate here. *The Exodus* was the outstanding success of the Makerere Travelling Theatre in 1965 wherever it was presented and has particularly excited many East African drama enthusiasts. Sympathetic readers in Britain, on the other hand, have received it coolly. One explanation may be that it is difficult to grasp the full depth of specifically epic material if one is totally unfamiliar with the social values from which it springs. Another may be that the verse form creates different, irrelevant expectations in the Westerner. People close to oral tradition may unselfconsciously adopt verse form when rhythmic tensions, however 'irregular', are felt very strongly. *The Exodus* may be related to and grow out of that different poetic manner which John Pepper Clark discusses in *Transition* 25: 'From the engendering of the word to its rendering as a poem, this is poetry that is delivered by mouth and aimed at the ear to move the whole body.'

The Makerere Travelling Theatre has presented plays in English, Swahili, Luganda, Lwo and Runyoro/Rutoro so far, varying the language medium within any one programme. A synopsis of plays in English is given verbally in Swahili and the local vernacular before each performance. Most of the plays in African languages have happened to be short comedies, and always bring the house down; but when village audiences without formal education have been asked which plays they liked best, the answer has almost invariably been the plays in English —because these plays were more serious and gave more food for thought. This is not, of course, specific evidence in favour of English—Julius Nyerere's translation of *Julius Caesar* very often outbids the English plays in popularity—but it does show that, appropriately presented, a play can surmount the language barrier; and a company restricted in its linguistic range can nevertheless convey the spirit and meaning of drama very widely.

Audience responses to several of the plays in this anthology have been interesting. An East African audience laughs not only at things which an average European spectator would recognize as 'funny', but also whenever it is surprised, especially if the surprise is under emotional tension. This is probably a universal human reaction which has been inhibited in recent centuries by European social conventions, except perhaps in the music hall and the circus. We all know that comic fulfilment causes us to laugh even when we foresee what is going to happen. An expected tragic death may also demand a release, which may just as well be expressed in laughter as in tears. A writer needs to allow for this, and even more so the producer, by the use of pauses and a calculated sequence of action which will enable the actor to quieten his excited hearers before they need to hear more of the text. Interestingly enough we found safeguards of this kind built into Shakespeare's text, which we had never detected before playing *Julius Caesar* to unsophisticated gatherings: clearly audiences in the Globe had much in common with African rural communities. It follows that a company should not mistake laughter at a dramatic climax for failure. One must learn to distinguish between delighted, awed, raucous, and self-protective laughter, and to predict where each kind may occur, so as to avoid it, or better still to shape and control it. In any case, East African social groups have amongst themselves varying social customs and conventions. An audience in Northern Uganda reacts differently from one which is predominantly Bantu. It is hard for a group of actors to realize that people who laugh less during a comedy may be reacting as sympathetically as those who laugh readily; but this may be the case in an area where unbridled laughter is frowned upon.

Laughter is not, of course, the only audience reaction to be reckoned with. Performers in organized drama must, by definition, be somewhat sophisticated people. Some East Africans will probably find themselves as shocked as Europeans when they first hear the non-stop burble of talk that greets any performance outside the walls of a theatre, school or college. It must rapidly be recognized that this chatter is about the play which is being acted, and is, indeed, an expression of positive, dynamic response and participation, to be welcomed not deplored.

The editors hope that this volume will be the beginning of an upsurge in the publication of East African drama. We are sure that there must be many playwrights we have not been lucky enough to contact so far. But we would always be happy to see manuscripts which have not previously come our way.

MILES LEE
DAVID COOK

Born to Die

SAM TULYA-MUHIKA

Characters in order of appearance

LAYERI
AYERI } sister fortune-tellers
STELLA   An educated girl
MAATHI DEHOTA   An educated man of thirty-five
A MOB OF PEOPLE
POLICE

Time 1962

> *A wooded hillside. As the curtain rises, progressively more and more light falls on the sister* FORTUNE-TELLERS, *who are seated on a mat, looking through their possessions, which include cowrie shells, a calabash containing beads, strange leaves, and a cow-horn.*

LAYERI (*looking at the sky*): Sister Ayeri, the sky is clear and hopeful tonight; the moon wears a well-cut smile. I can see a young man laden with ambition and great hopes who has lost his way and is groping about in the dark.

AYERI (*also looking up*): I don't see quite the same, Sister Layeri. Myriads of stars twinkle in silent whispers. The horizon is curved like a maiden's womb, and distant Mwanza hillocks stick up sharply like breasts on a virgin's chest. My guess would be a young woman.

LAYERI: You may be right, Sister Ayeri. (*Pause.*) I don't know how much longer we shall go on like this before we are over-run by Dehota and his murderous gang.

AYERI: I don't know, Sister Layeri. We are all marked to die sooner or later. I am getting tired of living in the bush. Dehota made us run away from a settled life only to die by inches. We ran away from sanity. We are all fugitives from sanity. But I believe it is quite safe hiding here. Oh, poor sisters!

LAYERI: Sssh . . . here comes someone.

Enter STELLA.

STELLA: I have come to have my fortune told.

AYERI: Come nearer, my child. Why do you tempt us to death?

STELLA (*approaching*): I am not tempting you. All I want is my future told. The light of my life is darkness: my last ray of hope has gone out, like a flicker in the dark. I won't go any further without knowing where I'm going, and I'm told you are fortune-tellers.

AYERI: My child, fortune-tellers can see the future in the past. But we are none.

LAYERI: We are two old women who have had all they didn't want in life and have taken to living in the hills like spirits.

AYERI: The three fortune-tellers I knew were murdered last week, brutally butchered.

LAYERI: Yes, they were run down by a mob, driven by a mad-man—a man by the name of Dehota who called himself a reformer.

AYERI: He incited the mob; he got them drunk with rage for murder; he filled them with words, with emptiness, with the opium of society.

LAYERI: They were gripped by mass drunkenness; so they went out to loot, to pillage, to strike, to murder, to destroy.

STELLA: You speak so passionately of these dead witches. The three deserved their end. They molested innocents and . . .

AYERI: You call them witches, do you? You may as well call us witches.

LAYERI: My child, they were mere soothsayers, ordinary fortune-tellers.

STELLA: No. They were fortune-tellers extraordinary. They bewitched innocents. Karu's child was born without any hands. Matiya's daughter died of a strange cough at the age of two. Haumi's three-year-old son turned red and earth-brown, his body swelled all over and he died. Makuru's cows were struck by dry lightning. Ngomi's children are catching a strange disease that makes their bodies and hair turn brown. How can I say everything?

AYERI: Mishaps happen, my child.

STELLA: Yes, but these were cases of witchcraft. Such infant deaths are unknown to our tribe. Anyway that is all past, and beyond recall. All I want is my future told. (*Pause.*) Dehota did not tell the mobs to murder. We are all more sensible than our actions suggest. He is a well-meaning reformer: he only advised the people against witches—quite rightly too!

LAYERI: Sister Ayeri, she says that it was right that our sisters be murdered with such ruthless brutality.

STELLA: Ah! They were your sisters, were they? That makes all the difference. I am sorry for you; your sisters were indeed brutally murdered. But then surely you are the fortune-tellers I'm looking for. For you see, all I want is my future told.

AYERI: We are no fortune-tellers of any merit.

STELLA: But you are fortune-tellers of sorts and all I want is my future told.

The FORTUNE-TELLERS *confer in whispers.*

AYERI: Can we depend on you?

STELLA: Yes, you can.

LAYERI: What assurance have we?

STELLA: You have the word of a young girl who has a whole past to regret.

LAYERI: Swear by the moon.

STELLA: I swear.

AYERI: And by the sun.

STELLA: I swear.

LAYERI: And by the heavens.

STELLA: I swear, I swear, by the moon, by the sun, and by the heavens.

AYERI: You see, my child, if we may confide in you, we ran away from our homes, ran away from Dehota and his mad crowd.

LAYERI: They trampled our innocent sisters to death, so we ran here. Even now we would be killed if we were discovered.

AYERI: That is why we made you swear. You aren't the only one; day in, day out, we are visited by a continual band of harassed people like you, all worried about the future—as if it was their concern.

STALLA: All I want is mine told.

LAYERI: Yes, my child, you look young and learned, fresh and just unleashed upon life.

AYERI: We are rustic, unread, and vulgar old hags: that is what you call us.

LAYERI: How can we know your future?

STELLA: I know you can tell my future, and it is vital that I have it told. My learning and my youth are no match for your tried experience. Young or old, learned or unread, rich or poor, big or small, we all live in the same world. We all live life: we are all tossed about by waves in this universal ocean. My future must be told.

AYERI: You are bent to know, my child. We shall tell you. What ails you?

STELLA: A lot, but one thing in particular. My problem is from within. I was fresh out of college with all my future before me, untapped. I looked forward to a good job, to being happily married to a lovable husband, delightful children to bring up, all the good things of life. Then I met a man bubbling with life and ideas. He was strong, but in strength lies weakness. He said he loved me, and I'm sure he did; so we went around together for days, weeks and months. I gave myself to him. Recently I discovered that I was different. I discovered that I was a woman, a mother.

LAYERI: Ah, my child, that sounds a familiar story. But what can we do about it?

STELLA: My trouble is not my illegitimate pregnancy. It is something worse. My man agreed we should get married. But before we could do so, he was accused of committing some criminal offence. Now he must flee the country as a death warrant has been issued for him: he can be shot on sight if he attempts to run. The police are combing the countryside for him.

AYERI: Maybe they won't catch him.

STELLA: Maybe they will catch him, or maybe he will run away and leave me alone. Oh, kind fortune-tellers, have compassion on me. You are women like me, and although you have grown old, and lost the fresh water of womanhood, you can feel what I feel. It is not my fault if I have a life to live. Oh for someone to marry me! My light is darkness. I have failed to possess myself; someone else must own me, and only he alone can salvage me from the ruins of my life.

AYERI: What do you want to know?

STELLA: I got carried away. All I want is my future told. I want to know whether my man will get caught or not, because if he does, the sentence is sure to be death, and then there will be no one to marry me with all my troubles.

AYERI: My child, we can't tell the future of someone we don't see.

LAYERI: He must come here himself and tell us all his past, and then we can tell him his future.

AYERI: Because the future is identical with the past.

STELLA: Well, I can tell you his past, that part of it is known to me.

AYERI: No, my child; he must tell us himself. Our oracle won't listen to anyone but himself.

STELLA: Oh, you crush my hopes. Where shall I go to have my future told?

MAATHI DEHOTA *has entered unseen during the previous speech. He is bearded and roughly dressed like a fugitive. His hair is ruffled.*

DEHOTA: I have come to have my future told.

They all turn in alarm.

STELLA (*rushing to him*): Oh Maathi! Maathi! How do you come to be here? It's impossible.

DEHOTA (*embracing her*): The impossible happens: nothing is so impossible that it can't happen.

STELLA: Oh, I'm so thrilled to see you. I was lost in this vast emptiness. You've come just at the right moment for me. Will they catch you? Are you running away? Is there hope for us together? Can we still be happy, Maathi? Can't you prove you are innocent?

DEHOTA: Stella, I can't answer all your questions; I can't answer any questions. No questions can be answered. No question has ever been answered. No, Stella, I can't prove my innocence. The truth is incredible: it is too true to be believed. I can't prove the truth; the law won't be appeased: it will crush me; I must run away from the law. (*To* STELLA) What are you doing here?

STELLA: Oh Maathi, I felt lonely. I felt lost. My life had no bearings without you. I wanted to know whether there was a future for us together. No-one would tell me. So I came here. Oh please don't leave me. Don't throw me to life all by myself. Life is a ravenous lion without you. It's a starved cormorant; it will devour me. You killed me: don't kill me again.

DEHOTA: Stella, you accuse me of murder; the police accuse me of murder; the air accuses me of murder. I am accused of murder wherever I turn. Whoever I look at is murdered later on in the day. The end is settled; I want to know how soon it is coming. (*Tearing himself free, to the* FORTUNE-TELLERS) I have come to have my future told.

STELLA: Oh Maathi! Maathi! Will they catch you? The police . . .

DEHOTA: Don't mention the police. (*To* FORTUNE-TELLERS) I want my future told.

AYERI: We tell no future but by the past.

DEHOTA: I know my past all right. It is not worth knowing.

AYERI: Then that is your future: that's what will happen.

DEHOTA: I want to hear more than that.

LAYERI: What do you want to happen to you?

DEHOTA: Old one, I don't know what to want. The more I get what I want, the more I don't want it. I find that what I want is only what part of me wants. To answer your question, I want to live on; to see more of life.

AYERI: But that is what you are doing.

DEHOTA: Not exactly; for the past week I have been living in the bush, in caves and holes like rats, eating nothing but what I came by, like a monkey. I have only been moving under the cover of darkness.

LAYERI: Why, my son, why?

DEHOTA: I am a fugitive from reality. I don't want to face what I've done: it is too overpowering for me.

LAYERI: My child, tell us something of your past.

DEHOTA: Old one, I have already told you my past is not worth knowing; certainly not worth listening to. At the age of twenty-five, after college, I set out to make a name in the world; I had great dreams for my tribe and for my country. I knew what was right and I knew the truth, but I overlooked the people. I set out to make marvellous reforms in society, and now, only ten years later, I am a fugitive from the right things I have done. I overlooked that the right is only right as long as it happens to be what the people want. Now I am a complete failure and all my marvellous plans have come to nothing.

AYERI: My child, unless you are more precise about your past, we cannot tell you your future.

DEHOTA: Be patient. I will tell you. I met this girl here. She was fair and loving . . .

LAYERI: She has told us about that side of your past.

STELLA: I have. Maathi, I had to. Was I wrong?

DEHOTA: No, Stella, you weren't. Anything is right, depending on who does it. (*To* LAYERI) Then you know all I want: I want my future told. Shall I succeed if I try to escape?

STELLA: Maathi, you don't intend to run away and leave me alone, do you? Won't you take me with you?

DEHOTA (*to* AYERI): Is there a future for me?

AYERI: Can we trust you?

DEHOTA: Yes, you can.

LAYERI: What assurance?

AYERI: Won't you give us away to Dehota?

DEHOTA: But I am Dehota—Maathi Dehota!

The FORTUNE-TELLERS *rise with piercing shrieks and try to run.* DEHOTA *seizes them. They shriek the more.*

DEHOTA: You shan't go. You shan't go until I hear my future.

AYERI: You're a murderer; let us go.

DEHOTA: I won't let you go until . . .

LAYERI: You want to kill us; you're a spy. You were tempting us. Let us alone.

DEHOTA: I am no murderer.

LAYERI: You are! Everybody says so. Let us go or else I will scream.

AYERI (*struggling to free herself*): Let me go or I'll scratch and kick you. I'll bite you. I'll tear your eyes out. I'll kill you. Let me go.

DEHOTA: I won't let you go to your death. I want to save you and if you sit down I'll tell you the truth.

AYERI: I don't want to hear the truth from a murderer. Save us? Ha! Let me go.

STELLA: Listen, listen; he didn't murder them.

AYERI: That's what you would say.

LAYERI (*to* DEHOTA): Leave me, let me alone, or else I'll jump onto your neck and squeeze life out of you.

STELLA: Gentle old women, we want to save you. If you run away, you may run into the mob and get killed. Sit down and listen to the truth.

AYERI: I won't have the truth from a madman, a murderer.

STELLA (*pulling* AYERI *down*): Sit down and stop being silly and obstinate. Does Maathi look like a murderer? Sit down and listen.

LAYERI: Sister Ayeri, shall we stay? This looks like the end. (AYERI *nods.*) Loosen your iron grip, innocent murderer. We shall stay.

He lets them go. They sit and eye him suspiciously.

DEHOTA: So often I have to do what I disapprove of; and it is so painful.

AYERI: You know I'd much rather you didn't talk about these sickening events. Anyway, what's your version of the truth?

DEHOTA: The truth is incredible. (*Pause.*) Listen, Stella here will confirm what I say. I am a reformer. I told the people not to believe in witches, but in science and Christianity. They lost their heads; they all poured out what they had suffered at the hands of life, and attributed it to the witches. They were gripped by emotion and madly resolved to go on a witch-hunt. I sensed from bitter experience that trouble was afoot, so I ran to the Chief in the village and told him. We came with askaris in a breathless hurry, but alas! we were too late. An old woman, alleged to be a witch, had been torn to death, and another was being pursued. The crowd was crazy and thoughtless, and I was to blame. But we miraculously saved the fleeing old woman.

AYERI (*to* LAYERI): It was Lubeire. (*To* DEHOTA) She came to warn us.

DEHOTA: Yes, that's the truth. This was not the first time crowds had got out of my control. At the Williamson Mines, I was a big man in a top post. I felt that some changes were needed, but before my negotiations were through, the workers grew impatient and started a riot. I lost my job. I had no better luck with East African Railways and Harbours. That's one side of my regrettable past. There is Susanna too. For many years we had an understanding that we would get married.

AYERI: My son, have you made a marriage promise to another girl besides this one?

DEHOTA: Yes, old one, Susanna was my first love. Poor girl!

LAYERI: You deserted her?

DEHOTA: Yes.

LAYERI: Why, my son?

DEHOTA: I needed someone who would help me in my plans to make this country a better place. Stella understood what I was striving for. She wanted to help. She could help.

AYERI: What about Susanna?

DEHOTA: She couldn't help. She wasn't open-minded enough. We met in our youthful days—at school. But she didn't go beyond the lower classes. And I went on, much longer.

LAYERI: Did that make any difference?

DEHOTA: Yes, old one. We could hardly talk the same language. And so I left her for Stella.

LAYERI: And then . . .

DEHOTA: When she discovered this, she was so overwhelmed that she killed herself. And now the police . . .

STELLA: The police have always worked against him. They don't understand.

DEHOTA: The police claim evidence that I murdered her to marry Stella.

STELLA: Can't you tell them that they are wrong? The police can be stupid at times.

DEHOTA: Stella, I have no chance to tell the police that they're wrong. I have no chance to show myself. The police are after me, to shoot me, to kill me, to save me the trouble of living.

AYERI: Why to shoot you, my son?

DEHOTA: They say I killed Susanna to marry Stella. They say I enflamed the crowd and am therefore guilty of the old woman's death. I am being hunted as a dangerous man.

LAYERI: Are the police not telling the truth?

AYERI: Our sister is dead. And Susanna is dead too.

LAYERI: Both because of you and your ideas.

DEHOTA: Old ones, I agree Susanna is dead. Poor girl! And your sister is dead. It is all a sad business. But I didn't kill them. It has never been in my mind to kill anybody.

LAYERI: What is your aim?

DEHOTA: My idea is to save people, not to destroy them.

LAYERI: My son, it is not easy to save people. Some people prefer not to be saved. Some of them are greyheads—older than you: you are too young.

DEHOTA: But, old one, I had a vision and I wanted to save them.

AYERI: Yours was a brave ambition, my son. But you cannot save people unless you understand them.

LAYERI: And unless they understand you.

AYERI: Fine ideas are not enough by themselves.

LAYERI: They are only a beginning.

AYERI: And if you put them into practice without really knowing what you're doing, they can be very dangerous, as you now know.

DEHOTA: Old ones, it is too late now to know anything that can change my destiny. I want to know only one thing from you. Will I escape the police?

LAYERI (*throwing up the cowries*): We shall tell you.

AYERI (*churning the contents of the calabash*): We shall tell you. Did you greet anybody on your way here?

DEHOTA: No.

AYERI: Do you wear a fetish?

DEHOTA: No, not since I went to school.

LAYERI (*throwing up cowrie shells*): That's a sign that you don't believe in good luck.

AYERI (*still churning*): How old are you?

DEHOTA: Thirty-five.

LAYERI (*shuffling the leaves*): Too young to live. Life is a long, long road, and the farther you go along it, the more you die. (*Throwing up cowries*) The more you die, the more you understand life; the more you die—the more you live.

DEHOTA: You may be right. But I prefer to live while I still have life. Am I born to die, like a mosquito? To spend my life dying?

LAYERI (*pointing to cowries*): This points northerly to Lake Victoria. Yes, you must die to live, and you must die while you are still alive. All my family died in the process of living. My poor husband died of starvation trying to escape from his regiment in World War Two. Poor man! He was barely identifiable when the body was found.

AYERI: My son was killed in the war, too, and three years later my only daughter died in childbirth. All went, leaving me a traveller lost in this trackless desert. (*She throws up the cowries.*) This points to the lake again.

DEHOTA: How long are you going to be doing that?

AYERI: We shall have no questions. Don't tell a butcher how to wear his skin.

LAYERI (*throwing shells aside*): Let me see your hands.

DEHOTA (*to* STELLA): Must I?

STELLA: Go, Maathi: of course you must; you must just do whatever they tell you.

He holds out his hands suspiciously. LAYERI *reaches out to touch them.* DEHOTA *withdraws.*

DEHOTA: Hey! Must you?

LAYERI: Yes, I must. Come, my child; you are not a murderer; and I am not a witch.

STELLA: Maathi, please! (*He holds out his hands again.*)

LAYERI (*fingering his hands*): There are breaks in the lines of your hands. That's a sure sign of bad luck in life.

STELLA: Mine have no faults, but I've had all the bad luck in the world.

DEHOTA: What is all this talk about luck for? All I want to know is whether I shall successfully dodge the police.

AYERI (*shaking calabash*): Patience, young man, patience.

LAYERI: Show patience, young man. (*She blows and listens into the horn.*) You've got the mark of fate grafted into you; you can't run away from it. (*She fiddles with the shells.*)

STELLA (*listening*): Sssh ... I can hear a noise.

All listen in alarm.

LAYERI: I can hear cows mooing; the herdsmen are out with their animals.

AYERI: I can hear a dog barking, something like a hound baying.

DEHOTA (*about to flee*): It's a police dog: they've got me.

STELLA (*holding him back*): Stay, dear, don't be silly. Police dogs don't bark. I shall go and look. (*She scans the distance.*)

DEHOTA: Of course police dogs don't bark; how stupid of me! You see, I'm so on edge, Stella. (*Alarmed*) What is it?

STELLA (*half shrieking*): People!

ALL: What?

The FORTUNE-TELLERS *rise.*

STELLA: People! With sweaty faces, carrying sticks, clubs and pangas, all wading their way through the bush up the hill.

DEHOTA (*rushing to look*): It's the crowd, the witch-hunters. (*To* FORTUNE-TELLERS) Quick! Quick! Run for your lives. They have smelt you! They have sensed you! They'll be here before one can say, 'Run away'.

STELLA: Will they kill the fortune-tellers?

DEHOTA: They might. (*To* FORTUNE-TELLERS) Run for it.

The FORTUNE-TELLERS *stagger out clumsily, crying and whimpering,
kicking everything over; they try to drag* MAATHI *with them, but*
STELLA *stands in their way. Enter a* CROWD *of men, women and
children, sweating and breathless, shouting madly and apparently
ruthless. They carry clubs, sticks, knives, hoes, mattocks and axes.*

1ST MAN: Where are they?

2ND MAN: Where are the witches?

3RD MAN: Where are the witches?

1ST MAN: Hang them!

2ND MAN: Quarter them!

3RD MAN: Tear them!

DEHOTA: There are no witches here.

2ND MAN: Don't try to hide them.

1ST MAN: My children are down with the red disease.

3RD MAN: All my cows are bewitched.

1ST MAN (*pointing to the cowries*): Hi! Look! They've just been here.

2ND MAN: The track's still fresh.

3RD MAN: Come on! Let's pursue them hot.

1ST MAN: Let's cut them off the face of Mwanza.

3RD MAN: Pursue them hot!

2ND MAN: Tear them apart!

1ST MAN: Hang them!

2ND MAN: Bury them alive!

3RD MAN: Gouge out their eyes!

1ST MAN: Rip out their evil hearts!

2ND MAN: Batter their withered bodies.

The whole CROWD *takes up the hue and cry and exits in pursuit.*

DEHOTA (*as the* CROWD *moves off*): Stop! Listen! Stop! (*He is thrown
violently aside.* STELLA *pulls him out of the crowd's track.*)

STELLA: Are you all right?

DEHOTA (*weakly*): Yes, dear. They'll murder them; the crowd
will tear the soothsayers to pieces.

STELLA: What can you do about it now? Think about yourself
and me. You and I must escape from this country to be happy

elsewhere. The police have offered a fabulous sum for any information leading to your arrest, and some of the crowd will surely talk.

DEHOTA: I'm sure you're right. But I mustn't take you with me. What have you done to leave your country, your motherland?

STELLA: Maathi, don't talk like that. Of course, if you must go, I must. We are part of each other.

DEHOTA: Look, Stella, you would only hinder my escape.

Part of the CROWD *re-enters.*

1ST MAN: That's fixed those two.

DEHOTA: What? Did you . . . What did you do to them?

1ST MAN (*proudly*): Found them hobbling up a crag like two drunken rats.

2ND MAN: We struck them down. They're both meat now, dinner for vultures—if they care to dig deep enough.

STELLA (*collapsing into* DEHOTA'*s arms*): Oh, what brutality!

DEHOTA: You! You're drunk with desire to murder. Who gave you the right to go around killing every old woman?

2ND MAN: They weren't old women: they were infernal witches and sorceresses.

3RD MAN: Witches engaged in divinations and enchantments.

DEHOTA: Are you the judges and the hangmen too?

2ND MAN: Listen, Dehota, we want to warn you. (*He holds up his club.*)

1ST MAN: The other three charged with you have been arrested and the police are hot on your track.

DEHOTA: Wha - a - at?

1ST MAN: They would have you now if we had not misdirected them at the bottom of the hill.

3RD MAN: I should fly if I were you.

2ND MAN: As for us, we shall hunt on.

They exit.

DEHOTA: Stay. Stay and tell me more. Which way did the police
go? (*No answer.*) They've gone. Let them go. Let them run
off. Maybe I was born to die.

STELLA: No, Maathi, you were not born to die; you were born
to marry me.

DEHOTA: Stella, how can you talk of marriage? Can't you see
that I'm caught in a whirlpool?

STELLA: The more reason why you need me, then. You need
someone to warm your heart; to caress you all over and make
you forget your troubles. We must go together.

DEHOTA: But you have no cause for flight. Don't think like a
woman.

STELLA: But I am a woman.

DEHOTA: Yes, but I'm telling you not to think like one. This is a
situation for men. I must go alone; it makes more sense.

STELLA: Not to me. Maathi, I've failed to possess myself; you
must possess me. How can you leave me alone?

DEHOTA: How can you come with me? You have no idea what
dangers and dark hours lie ahead.

STELLA: Dangers or no dangers, you must take me. Who would
marry me if you left me? I would be tossed about by men
like chaff. You couldn't go alone; you wouldn't be complete.
(*Pointing to her womb*) Part of you is here.

DEHOTA: I must fly fast. This talking is only delaying my flight.
If you feel so helpless without me, come along then. (*He
urges her forward.*)

STELLA: Wait, Maathi, I must collect my possessions first.

DEHOTA (*as she is going*): Where will you find me?

STELLA: Here, under this tree, the tree of promise.

DEHOTA: I don't want you to go and not to find me on your
return.

STELLA: But I'll be back in no time, Maathi.

They embrace and separate.

DEHOTA: Go then, Stella. Leave me here; hurry and be back

in no time. (*To himself*) I have played my part, my contribution. After all, I'm only a man.

Exit STELLA. *The light dims.*

As for the rest, I shall pray to God. (*He follows her off-stage with his eyes.*) That's her: curly hair, firm shoulders, feminine pace . . . She is going and I am staying. (*He paces up and down.*) That parting sounds so final. I wonder whether I shall ever see her again. (*Pause.*) The fortune-tellers, why were they killed? Were they witches? Their blood cries loud behind me —nobody can hear what I want to say. Yet I didn't kill them. Susanna too! She lost her nerve and ended her life. Was it because of me? Oh, I'm haunted; I feel guilty. And the police! Do they understand what they're doing? I can see countless police eyes looking for me—not to see me, but to see my guilt. I can feel their hands tipped with death all closing in upon me. (*He gesticulates wildly.*) The glaring eyes of a High Court judge, and then the hangman's cord! God! (*In an altered tone*) Life has always surprised me. The whole affair of living stinks of regular irregularity, like a fool's dance. Wherever I go I find that right is wrong. Wherever I go I find problems. Is it possible that I am the problem? (*Pause.*) What's the answer?—the solution?

Enter the POLICE *from all directions. They advance threateningly on* DEHOTA. *They act in unison with stylized movements.*

DEHOTA: It's you! You're too late. I am not much to kill: I've spent my life dying.

The POLICE *close in upon him. He collapses heavily to the ground.* STELLA *breaks in.*

STELLA: Maathi! Maathi! Maathi!

Curtain

Undesignated

KULDIP SONDHI

Characters

MRS SAVITRI GURU
MR PREM GURU
MRS KAMLA PATEL
MR RAJINDER PATEL
MR MAJID
MR SOLOMON OHANGA
MISS JUNE MWENDWA
MR WABERA

Scene 1. The living-room of PREM GURU's *house.*
Scene 2. The flat of SOLOMON OHANGA, *next day.*

Scene 1

It is around 7 p.m. and PREM *and his wife are putting the last touches to their living-room in preparation for a cocktail party.*

SAVITRI *is standing by the drinks table arranging flowers in a silver vase.* PREM *is filling up the cigarette boxes which lie on the occasional tables.*

On the up stage wall of the room hangs an oil painting which depicts an African scene. It is blazing with colour.

The room is comfortably furnished in Indian middle-class, Western fashion.

The front door of the house leads directly into the living-room and there is another door or archway which leads to the rest of the house.

MRS GURU: Now Prem, the Minister comes tonight and you must stand for your rights.

PREM: Let's not go over that again, Savitri.

MRS GURU: No, but I just want you to remember that tonight is very important.

PREM (*glancing at his watch*): Solomon and the others should be arriving any moment now. (*Straightens painting on wall. Knock on door.* MRS GURU *nods to* PREM *to answer and leaves through inside door.* PREM *opens door.* MR *and* MRS RAJINDER PATEL *enter.*)

PREM: Come in, come in (*returns folded hands greeting to* MRS RAJINDER).

RAJINDER: Good evening sir. Are we the first to come? (*Sees painting on wall and walks over to it immediately.*)

PREM (*to* MRS RAJINDER): Savitri is in the kitchen, Kamla.

MRS RAJINDER: I will go and help her. (*Leaves through inside door.*)

PREM (*smiles as he sees* RAJINDER'S *preoccupation*): It had the same effect on me when I saw it at the G.M.'s house.

RAJINDER (*half turning when he hears this*): How did he get it, I mean did you get it from him, sir?

PREM: The G.M.'s collected a lot of material after twenty years in Kenya. But he can't take everything back with him to England. Good of him to give this to me. (*He walks over and hands his junior a drink. Both men stand studying the painting. Then* PREM *peers forward and adjusts his spectacles in an elderly gesture.*) Still haven't been able to make out who did it. Can you read the name, Rajinder?

RAJINDER (*starting when he hears this and looking closer himself*): Yes, you are quite right, sir. It isn't signed. I'm not surprised though.

PREM: Oh?

RAJINDER: May I make a suggestion?

PREM: Of course.

RAJINDER: Please remove it from your wall.

PREM: What!

RAJINDER: I know who did it. He works for you. But it will make him very unhappy if he sees it here tonight. Especially tonight.

PREM: What on earth are you talking about?

RAJINDER: May I be quite frank, sir?

PREM: For heaven's sake, man! (*He looks puzzled at the younger man, who is earnest, spectacled, about thirty-three.*)

RAJINDER: I wasn't actually there when it was done but I know the man very well. A fine man. A great artist . . . but something went wrong, I suppose. (*Keying himself to take the plunge as he paces the front of the stage.*)

PREM: Well?

RAJINDER: Solomon was with me at Cambridge—

PREM: Solomon Ohanga?

RAJINDER: Yes. We shared digs. But I never really understood Solomon. It was months before I discovered quite by chance that he had already been in Europe for three years before we met. He spent that time painting and wandering all over the continent, going wherever fancy took him.

PREM: Solomon Ohanga, our transport engineer, the hope of the department, the man considered most likely to succeed, a wandering painter. I can't believe it, Raj!

RAJINDER: It's quite true, sir.

PREM: Of course.

RAJINDER: I questioned him one day after we got friendly. He became agitated and told me that he had tried to live on the sale of his painting in Europe, but found it impossible, so he returned home. Here someone offered him an engineering scholarship and he took it. He is a clever man, nothing special as an engineer perhaps, but he got through like any of us. I'm sorry, sir, if any of this shocks you.

PREM: No, that's all right . . . hmmmm! Is all this true?

RAJINDER: Every word. I know how hard it is to believe, especially since Solomon never talks about his past. He would be very upset at seeing any of his paintings again, especially here and today.

PREM: Especially today as you say. . . . Well, well, Solomon Ohanga! Don't think I don't appreciate what you have told me but this complicates the whole situation. You have just precipitated a crisis in the Transport Ministry. Do you realize that?

RAJINDER: I think the others are coming, sir.

PREM: What. . . . Oh quick! Let's take it down before the situation gets more complicated. I don't want my wife to know any of this, either. (*He pulls up a chair and takes down the painting hurriedly.* RAJINDER *takes it from him.*)

RAJINDER: But the secret's quite safe. No one else knows except—

PREM (*standing down*): Except who?

RAJINDER: Except his fiancée.

PREM: Hmmmm (*glancing at him somewhat suspiciously*) what else is there that I should know. Careful now . . . let's not damage it . . . well, well! (*Sound of ladies returning from inside room, through door leading to interior.* PREM *and* RAJINDER *look desperately for a hiding place, finally slip painting behind the drink sideboard, as ladies enter.*)

MRS GURU: Hello, Raj; where are the others? (*With a glance at his wife*) You are a lucky man. (*Catches sight of empty place on wall. Her husband nods back vigorously. There is a knock on the front door.*)

PREM (*tense*): Yes; come in, Solomon! (*Door opens. A tall athletically built man of about thirty-two walks in.*) Oh it's you, Majid.

MAJID (*rubbing hands together and bowing to ladies. Strong British accent*): Good evening ladies, good evening sir. Am I too early or is it all over (*laughs at his own joke and continues talking*) . . . the others are just behind. I passed Solomon in his new Mercedes. Preparing himself, I suppose!

RAJINDER (*scarcely concealing his mistrust for the man*): Have a drink, Majid. What can I get you?

MAJID: Whisky soda, old man.

MRS GURU (*smiling*): And how's your tennis getting on these days?

MAJID: Oh quite well, you know, very well in fact thank you! I should reach the semi-finals at least this year. (*Rubbing hands again and winking at everyone in general.*) Good sport you know. Might even go further with a little luck. Did you know, sir, that Solomon has also taken up tennis?

PREM (*interested*): Oh indeed?

RAJINDER (*behind drink table drily*): So have I.

MAJID: That's different.

RAJINDER: What's so different about it? Tennis is tennis, nothing more or less.

MAJID: It's exercise for you, but prestige for him, like the new Mercedes he's just bought. But he won't get away with it!

RAJINDER (*curious, handing him his drink*): What do you have in mind?

MAJID (*looking around conspiratorially*): I suppose I can say it in present company. A number of engineers in the department and I have decided to draw up a petition protesting against any appointment to the top position other than yourself, sir. (*Looking at deputy general manager*, PREM) Fair's fair!

PREM: But—

MRS GURU: Let the young man finish, Prem. This is a democracy!

MAJID: And that's exactly what I say! If it's a democracy, then fair's fair.

RAJINDER: And who is going to pay any attention to this petition?

MAJID: The higher authorities of course, the Government, old man. (*Bitingly*) People who count.

PREM: Now Majid—

MRS GURU: And what are you going to say in your petition?

MAJID: I propose making the situation very clear. It isn't cricket.

RAJINDER: I thought it was tennis.

MAJID: The wording of the petition will be left to me, of course, and what I propose saying will leave no doubts in the minds of the Government how we feel in·this affair!

PREM (*firmly*): I don't want you to go any further with this, Majid; I know you mean well but no good will come of it. The Government already made up its mind over policy and your petition won't help at all.

MAJID (*protesting*): But delivered in the right places it's bound to help, sir.

PREM (*shaking his head but interested*): Who is in with you in this petition?

MAJID (*confident*): Most of the engineers in the transport and engineering section. People without whom the roads and railways would be paralysed.

RAJINDER: That means mostly Indians.

MAJID: I'm proud to be an Indian, old man!

PREM: So am I, so are we all, but we must bow to the will of the majority. They want an African in the top position and quite frankly I can see their point. (RAJINDER *nods in complete agreement.*)

MRS GURU: I think what Majid means is that there is no substitute for experience in a position of such importance.

MAJID: Exactly, madam! And that is what I propose saying in the petition. If there is an African or ... anyone for that matter to match the D.G.M. (*nodding deferentially towards* PREM) in experience and ability then well and good. But there isn't! Certainly not Mr Solomon Ohanga!

PREM: I repeat—

MRS GURU (*sweetly*): The Government might pay attention to your petition if it is well worded. I suppose there are many other civil servants in similar positions.

MAJID (*smiling confidently*): The Government will not be able to ignore what we say. The whole world is watching and listening to Kenya.

PREM (*shaking his head*): The world has nothing to do with this.

It's simply a question of choosing the right man to replace the retiring head of our transport department. That's all.

MAJID: More than that, sir. Principles are at stake . . . It's you today and me tomorrow!

RAJINDER: The D.G.M. has twenty years experience besides being an eminent engineer. There's a big difference beween him and you!

MAJID: Exactly! Imagine how much quicker we'd be axed.

RAJINDER: I accept Africanization. It's bound to succeed. No one thought the Suez canal would continue functioning when the Egyptians took over, but it's better than ever now.

MAJID: Egyptianization, my dear fellow, really started with the Pharaohs five thousand years back.

RAJINDER (*retorting*): And India became independent only fifteen years back. None of this has anything to do with your petition which I for one won't sign.

PREM (*stoutly*): Quite right!

MAJID (*rocking on his feet and looking over shoulder*): I believe he comes!

There is an air of expectation in the room when the knock comes. RAJINDER *moves over quickly and opens the door. A smart young African lady walks in first. She is followed by a tall, well-built man of about thirty-five. There is a good-natured, unmistakably refined air about him. He holds his hands Indian fashion, seeing the ladies.* MRS GURU *returns the greeting with a sweet smile.*

PREM: Come in, Solomon. Nice of you to have come.

SOLOMON: Good evening, sir. Sorry I'm late. The car gave some trouble. This is my fiancée, June Mwendwa.

PREM: I've heard of you, June. I'm glad he brought you along finally.

JUNE: It isn't his fault really. For the past six months I've been away with my parents in Uganda. (*She moves over to the ladies and shakes hands with them both.*)

MRS GURU: How nice to see you, June. Are you from America?

JUNE: No, I'm a Muganda really. I suppose one must still talk of tribes and all that though it's all silly in my opinion.

PREM (*nodding appreciatively*): How right you are! Now what can I offer you both to drink?

JUNE: A small sherry for me, please.

SOLOMON: I'll stand by Tusker if it's available.

MAJID (*hurrying over to drink table*): Let me get them, sir.

MRS GURU (*to* JUNE): Have you lived long in Kenya, June?

JUNE: Not very long, Mrs Guru. No more than a year in all.

MAJID: I can see she has spent years abroad.

SOLOMON (*laughing ruefully*): That she certainly has. I met her in England after she had returned from her studies in Massachusetts.

MRS GURU (*sweetly*): You must find Kenya very dull after England and your travels abroad.

JUNE: No place need be dull if one has true friends, Mrs Guru. (*Accepts drink from* MAJID.) Thank you, but I loved England and America.

MAJID: Hear! Hear! I am sure you did.

SOLOMON: I had some tough times there but all in all, I can't say I really suffered—thank you. (*Accepts drink from* MAJID.)

MRS GURU: You've not seen our house before, June. Would you like to see it now?

JUNE: I'd love to.

SOLOMON: Teach her how to cook curry as well, Mrs Guru. No amount of Africanization will make me like Indian food any less.

All laugh. Ladies exit inside door. MAJID *offers* SOLOMON *a cigarette.*

MAJID: What went wrong with your car? I passed you on the round-about. Did you see me?

SOLOMON: No I didn't. I suppose you went by at your usual speed.

MAJID: Anyhow my car can't really touch a new Mercedes.

RAJINDER: New?

SOLOMON: No, it's second hand and actually it's June's. She bought it with some money her father gave her when she returned from England.

MAJID: Good for her!

PREM: She's a fine young lady. When are you getting married?

SOLOMON: Tomorrow if she'd agree. But she won't just yet.

MAJID: Maybe she's waiting till you get promoted. You'll be able to afford a new Mercedes then!

SOLOMON (*good naturedly joining in the laughter*): Maybe you're right.

PREM: Good cars those. The Germans are first-rate engineers. I have the greatest respect for their abilities.

RAJINDER: You have made a number of original designs yourself, sir. Wasn't it one of their heavy trucks that incorporated your improvement on differential gearing?

PREM (*laughing*): Oh, that was many years back now. But I believe they used it in locomotives instead. (*Becomes reflective. Others keep respectfully quiet.*) I remember at the time we were busy working out the alignment of a new curve at Ulu and establishing repair services in up-country shops. Our present G.M. was an engineer like you young men are today. All this goes back twenty years. Time flies you know. Why . . . (*shakes his head reflectively and sighs*) well, there you are. All I have I've given to the Ministry and I hope they are satisfied.

SOLOMON: The Minister met me at a party yesterday, sir. He spoke about you. I assure you that he shares everyone's views. The department wouldn't be the same without you.

PREM (*moved*): Why, thank you, Solomon. You know I've enjoyed every single moment of my service. I only hope you youngsters will keep up the kind of team spirit we old-timers had.

Respectful laughter and wagging of heads.

MAJID: What party was this Solomon?

SOLOMON: A private party given by Dennis Githari. As you know he's recently been promoted to chief administrative officer for the Nairobi Repair Section.

MAJID: Yes, of course, Mr Githari is now my boss.

RAJINDER: And mine.

PREM: A very clever man, Dennis Githari. Risen from the ranks but equal to the best. A pity he had no formal education. On the other hand I don't know. . . .

SOLOMON: Yes, I felt the same way on meeting Dennis at close quarters. There's a certain earthy strength about the man that education might have sapped. And that's his chief quality, I think.

MAJID: His lack of education? (*Shrugs to soften the insinuation.*) Well, I mean that's what it sounds like.

RAJINDER: Dennis might not have our education but he has something else none of us have.

MAJID: And what could that be?

RAJINDER: Confidence of the people. Not just those who work directly under him now but the others, the ordinary linesmen and repairshop-men, who know him by first name.

MAJID: I wish I hadn't gone to school.

SOLOMON (*laughing*): But you have, of course, so you'll never be like Dennis Githari.

MAJID (*smiling but deadly*): The same applies to you, or doesn't it?

SOLOMON (*startled*): What? Oh well, yes of course.

MAJID: But surely the whole idea of higher education is to be able to hold some top post?

RAJINDER: Of course not!

PREM: Surely the whole idea of any education is to serve your fellow men.

MAJID: Oh yes, of course, that goes per se. But I mean, let's face it, an uneducated man can't really be expected to do what an educated man can do just as an inexperienced man can't be expected to do what an experienced man can do.

SOLOMON: Yes, you're right there. There isn't any real substitute for experience.

MAJID: Then you agree!

SOLOMON (*surprised*): But of course.

RAJINDER: Everyone agrees there isn't any substitute for experience, unless it be genius.

PREM: A genius can't remain hidden for long.

MAJID (*laughing*): I wonder if there isn't a genius among us?

SOLOMON: Must be you!

MAJID: Oh, no! We all know it's you!

SOLOMON (*shrugging lightly*): I'm just a simple engineer.

MAJID: Oh, you aren't and you know it, old man. You're a genius!

SOLOMON (*good-natured*): All right so I'm a genius. What does that make you?

MAJID: A non-designated transport engineer.

All laugh.

SOLOMON: For a moment I thought you were going to tell us what genius means.

MAJID: I intend doing that too. The genius in Kenya is the man who gets induced into service so that he gets an inducement allowance and designated to some service which makes him a designated officer and finally gets recruited overseas by interviewing someone in Nairobi!

SOLOMON (*laughing loudly*): The Minister would love that!

PREM: Designations and overseas allowances are all things of the past. You young men should forget all that now. There was a need for them once but that's all over.

MAJID: With respect, sir, I disagree. I only gave you half my definition of genius, Solomon.

SOLOMON: Oh?

MAJID: The real genius in Kenya today is the educated black man. By mere virtue of his colour and education he can secure any top job he wants. In fact there aren't enough available for the jobs that need them.

SOLOMON: Are you saying that there is something wrong in a black African getting a top post?

MAJID: You are putting words in my mouth, Solomon.

SOLOMON: Sorry, I didn't mean to do that, but I'm not quite clear what you are driving at?

MAJID: I was born here—

RAJINDER (*interrupting*): So was he, so was the D.G.M., so was I.

MAJID: In that case why isn't there equal opportunity for all of us. I was a second class citizen under the British. Am I to remain a second class citizen under the African Government as well?

SOLOMON: I was a third class citizen under the old Government. I won't be that any more and I'm sure you won't be either.

MAJID: But we can't be equal either, can we?

SOLOMON: That depends on the individual obviously.

MAJID: It doesn't and you know it! (*Getting excited*) Because if it did then why, why . . . pardon me bringing you into it, sir, but why, Solomon, why isn't our own superior, the D.G.M., being offered top post now that it's vacant and why aren't the others, men like me for instance, being given equivalent promotion?

SOLOMON (*laughing shortly*): I'm sure I don't know, Majid. I'm in the service like you; I hope you aren't going to hold me personally responsible for anything.

PREM: Of course not, my boy. Certain things are undoubtedly going to happen in this country, indeed are happening now, but it's only inevitable. No one is personally responsible for them. I accept the situation.

RAJINDER: So do I.

MAJID: Well I don't. (*Standing astride in the centre of the stage.*) Solomon I want you to understand me clearly. I was born here. I live here. I shall continue to live here. But if I do so I expect equal opportunity. I don't want to be treated like some member of a minority.

SOLOMON: But you are one, Majid. That's just a fact of nature.

No, let me finish now that you've started it. There is such a thing as a majority in a country and there is such a thing as majority representation in any country. That's the essence of democracy. If it isn't then I don't know what is. Justice hinges on that but if the Minister asked me for instance who was the best man fitted out for top job there isn't any doubt in your mind, I hope, whom I would mention. I feel no different to you, man. What do you think I am?

MAJID: You can afford to say all this, of course.

RAJINDER (*wagging an angry finger at him*): I'm going to be very frank about you in a minute, Majid. I am warning you!

MAJID (*shouting*): Well let's be frank for once then! You know as well as I who's going to be the next G.M. It isn't me or you or the D.G.M. It's him! (*Going to* SOLOMON.)

Stunned silence at his outburst. SOLOMON *stands frowning, apart.*

PREM: That's enough, Majid. I won't hear any more of this.

RAJINDER (*struggling for words*): Do you know that Solomon and I are very close to one another? He is a just man and there are things that he can do that none of us can, but I won't say it now. The difficulty with you is . . . you are just jealous!

MAJID: Don't be ridiculous. I have no personal grudge against Solomon. We play tennis together. But I don't suppose you would understand that.

SOLOMON (*glancing at them both and then smiling again with a shrug*): It's true what Raj says. We do know just about everything about each other. I owe him a lot. We were at Cambridge together. (*Shakes his head looking away.*) What days those were. I lived . . . yes, I lived like I won't ever now.

Ladies return, JUNE *leading.*

PREM: Come in, my dear. I think we can all do with another drink now.

JUNE: What a wonderful house, Mr Guru. And the view must be terrific.

MRS GURU: Come here sometime in the day, June, and I can show you the gardens as well.

JUNE: Thank you. That would be lovely, Mrs Guru.

PREM (*pouring one drink and then holding up depleted whisky bottle with grimace to his wife, then shaking his head*): That's all right, I know where it is. I'll get it.

PREM goes inside through door.

SOLOMON: Raj just reminded me of Cambridge again, June.

JUNE: Oh did he?

MAJID: He did and I called Solomon a genius, but he refuses to acknowledge it!

JUNE: What?

RAJINDER: One day, Majid, you will eat those words.

MAJID: I wish I were the genius.

JUNE: But genius in what?

SOLOMON: For being a black African at the right moment.

JUNE (*aghast*): Good lord!

MAJID (*protesting*): I didn't accuse you of that, Solomon—be fair man, I simply stated a fact. As the bard says, some are born into it and others have it thrust on them. With me for instance it's neither. I'll remain true to my own genius which is to be a non-designated transport engineer all my life!

SOLOMON (*nodding*): We must all be true to ourselves, each one of us. With me it's patriotism that comes first.

JUNE (*surprising everyone*): I disagree, Solomon. Your own true convictions must come first.

MAJID: A Daniel come to judgement—hear, hear!

SOLOMON: But patriotism is my true conviction.

JUNE: We are all patriotic, I hope.

MRS GURU: I agree with you, June. One's convictions must come first. You live by them. Two men with totally different views of life can be equally patriotic.

JUNE: That's exactly what I mean!

MAJID: Oh Daniel!

RAJINDER (*to* MAJID *quietly*): Her name is June.

SOLOMON: I want to do what's good for my country.

PREM (*returning with bottle*): Arguing again?

MAJID: Would you define patriotism for us, sir?

PREM (*going to the sideboard and pouring drinks*): Patriotism, well hmmm, let me see? Whisky, Majid, same for you, Raj, and soft drinks for the ladies, well yes, let me ... I would say that true patriotism can only come through the adherence to one's own principles and through that a realization of your country's greatest good.

JUNE: That I agree is the heart of the matter. And frankly I don't see how anyone could disagree with it.

RAJINDER (*accepting his drink and sipping thoughtfully*): True.

MAJID (*taking his drink notices the canvas leaning against the sideboard, lifts it for a view and whistles*): Well!

PREM (*hurriedly*): Yes, that's very good. I got it as a present.

MAJID: Now there's someone with principles. It shows his view of life and it's patriotic to the last drop of African blood!

JUNE: What is it?

MAJID (*holding up picture and showing it to her*): This.

JUNE (*gasps and puts hand across her mouth*): Oh!

SOLOMON (*stoical, having seen it*): It's quite good.

MAJID: Quite good? Why man, if you could do anything half as good as that you would be a genius!

As they are talking and looking at the painting a short thick-set, well-dressed man enters quietly from the outside door. MRS GURU *immediately sweeps past everyone to greet him.*

MRS GURU: Come in, Mr Wabera. So nice of you to have come.

MR WABERA (*shaking hands*): I'm so sorry for being late, Mrs Guru. I was at a meeting. (*Nods to* PREM.) Hello Prem. (*Then bows slightly to ladies in room.*) Good evening.

PREM: You all know the Minister, do you?

SOLOMON: I don't think you have met my fiancée, Mr Wabera?

MR WABERA: No, I haven't. Is that her?

SOLOMON: Yes. Miss June Mwendwa.

JUNE: How do you do, Mr Wabera. (*Goes up and shakes hands with* MINISTER.)

MR WABERA: You are not by any chance related to chief Mwendwa of Uganda?

JUNE: He is my father.

MR WABERA: Well, this is an honour, Miss Mwendwa. (*Adressing others*) Her father is one of Uganda's most famous chiefs. A great traditionalist and a great patriot.

MAJID: How would you define a patriot, Mr Wabera?

Others protest: Now Majid!

MR WABERA: Not at all—

PREM: Before you go into that, whisky and soda, John?

MR WABERA: Yes thank you, Prem. That would be fine. Lots of soda. Patriotism, well ... a most interesting question. A patriot I would say is a man who through his own actions satisfies and obeys the will of the people. No, that's not enough. A great patriot is not an imitator. He is a creator. So I would add that he is also a man of strong personal convictions. Yes, (*thinking aloud*) it follows I think and that is why you will find in any country that the real leaders are men chosen not so much for their personal brilliance as men who command the allegiance and love of the people because of the way they have fought and lived for their principles.

PREM (*chuckling*): I think that settles the argument.

RAJINDER *has used this time to whisk away the painting discreetly and slip it behind the sideboard.*

MR WABERA (*surprised*): Oh, was there another viewpoint on patriotism?

MAJID: Not on patriotism, sir, but the talk all began on what kind of man would be best suited to occupy, say, a top position in an important Government department.

Tense silence in room. Only MRS GURU *wears her sweet smile.*

MR WABERA (*blandly*): In a department like ours, for instance? Well of course the same rules apply. The head must be a man whom people accept and recognize as one of themselves and yet he must be a leader.

MAJID: Racially?

MR WABERA: Race is a fact. We cannot be blind to it.

SOLOMON: I agree.

MAJID (*controlling himself*): But, excuse me for saying this Mr Wabera, but a democracy must be blind to race.

MR WABERA: A democracy must be. Yes I agree.

SOLOMON: Quite right, sir. When we are a democracy that will happen.

RAJINDER: I agree with what you have said.

MAJID (*with a short laugh*): Then I represent the minority viewpoint.

MR WABERA (*blunt but friendly*): You do, but provided you help us it will make no difference in our feelings of friendship for you.

SOLOMON (*heatedly*): Democracy does not follow automatically with freedom. It must be created.

MAJID (*very personal and half mocking*): Of course!

JUNE (*glancing at her watch*): We will be late for the show, Solomon.

SOLOMON (*recovering*): Yes, I quite forgot.

PREM (*explaining*): Solomon is taking his colleagues out to a show at the National Theatre this evening. Celebrating June's arrival, I believe.

MR WABERA (*glancing at his watch*): You won't think me very rude, Mrs Guru, if I excuse myself as well. The show I must attend is somewhat different and probably not as entertaining.

All laugh.

MR WABERA (*holding out his hand to* JUNE): It's been a great pleasure meeting you, Miss Mwendwa. No doubt we will meet again. But meanwhile do convey my respects to your great father.

JUNE: Thank you. It will be a pleasure. (*Shakes hands with* MINISTER. MINISTER *and* PREM *leave first.* RAJINDER *and* SOLOMON *follow* MRS RAJINDER *and* JUNE *after thanking* MRS GURU. MAJID *leaves last.* MRS GURU *smiles at him as he leaves. There is the sound of a car starting outside.*)

MAJID (*suddenly poking his head back*): I wonder when I'll get my Mercedes. Goodbye, Mrs Guru.

MRS GURU *smiles at him again as he disappears. Then she stands alone on stage and starts clearing the table.* PREM *returns. He looks relaxed. His wife is silent for a moment before she speaks now.*

MRS GURU (*clearing bottles from the table helped by her husband*): Majid has courage.

PREM: I don't know about courage. He is certainly obstinate.

MRS GURU: Well he knows how to fight for his rights anyhow.

PREM: Sometimes it's better if you don't fight so hard.

MRS GURU (*her sweetness now all gone*): That's been the difficulty with you all your life—not standing up for yourself. Look at the way that upstart Solomon is trying to rob you of your position.

PREM (*defensively*): He is not trying to rob me of anything. It just happens that he is an African at the right time. I don't grudge him that.

MRS GURU: You don't grudge anything. If someone came tomorrow and said they wanted this house you would hand it over. I know you!

PREM: Well what do you want me to do? Come on, you tell me then!

MRS GURU: All I know is that the general managership is yours by right now. By every right under the sun. If you don't get it, it will be a sin.

PREM: We have had a good life in this country, Savitri. It's been very kind to us. I don't see why you are shouting.

MRS GURU: And you think you would have been a beggar in another country, a man of your brains and ability. I hate that man Solomon! And look what a mess the room has got into. Why was that picture taken down anyhow? Where is it now?

PREM: It . . . well . . .

MRS GURU: I suppose all this has something to do with the great Solomon Ohanga. And as for that girl of his, June— (*mimicking*) true friends, Mrs Guru—my God!

PREM (*taking out painting from behind sideboard*): All right, all right, Savitri. But she is a nice girl.

MRS GURU: Nice girl? My God! She knows what she wants, not like you! But why don't you talk to the Minister even now? Let him know your views.

PREM: In things like this the Minister must follow policy. He isn't really his own master. No one is.

MRS GURU: If we had a few more Majids in this country, things would be different for us.

PREM: They would! But I'm afraid you haven't understood Majid fully. I don't think he means everything he says and I don't think he is honest either.

MRS GURU: Don't be stupid now.

PREM: You're losing your temper again, Savitri.

MRS GURU (*leaving with tray*): Only my temper. Not our whole future like you're going to do.

MRS GURU *exits with tray.*

PREM (*replaces painting on wall. Stands down looking at it. Phone rings*): Hello . . . yes, Minister, go ahead. I'm completely alone—yes—yes, I understand—yes—

Curtain

Scene 2

SOLOMON's *flat. A lounge with small paintings hung on the walls and a picture of mount Kenya on one wall by itself. The settees and decor are colourful, light, modern.* SOLOMON *and* JUNE *are by themselves. Both look tense and wary.* SOLOMON *is seated, going through a magazine.* JUNE *is standing, looking away. Then she turns to him.*

JUNE: Did you enjoy the play last night?

SOLOMON: Yes I did.

JUNE: All the others did.

SOLOMON: So did I.

JUNE: You weren't even listening. How could you have enjoyed the play?

SOLOMON (*looking at her quickly*): How do you mean, I wasn't even listening? I enjoyed it immensely!

JUNE: I never heard you laugh once.

SOLOMON: Oh? (*Clutches head in his hands and gives up pretence.*) June, what are you trying to get at? Stop beating around the bush. You're an educated woman!

JUNE: And you are more than an educated man, so stop lying to yourself and to me!

SOLOMON (*raising his head and looking at her uneasily*): What does that mean?

JUNE: Why didn't you acknowledge your own work when you saw it yesterday at Mr Guru's house.

SOLOMON (*trying to laugh it off*): Oh, a small thing like that. I remembered it of course. It was done in England and later on I left it at a pawnbrokers. Amazing how it reached back here finally.

JUNE (*not listening to him*): Even the hardened Mr Majid saw the genius in it. Did you hear what he said?

SOLOMON (*dejected*): Yes but that part of my life is over.

JUNE (*getting excited*): Stop being such a fool Solomon. That part of your life has hardly begun. You've tried to escape from yourself but you can't. The mere sight of that painting upset you for the evening and still haunts you.

SOLOMON (*unhappily*): Well, what do you want me to do? Laugh and jump with joy!

JUNE: No, I don't want you to do an ngoma. But I do want you to stop lying to yourself. I want you to acknowledge the truth.

SOLOMON (*quietly*): And what is this truth that I am to acknowledge to myself?

JUNE: That it was a mistake for you to become an engineer because you are not cut out to be one. You are an artist. Not just a minor talent. But a man carrying in him and hiding a great gift. For how long can you hide it?

SOLOMON: June would you stop talking any more about the past? I want to forget it. I am an engineer now and the department needs me.

JUNE: You mean you need the department!

SOLOMON: Are we going to start shouting at each other?

JUNE: Yes, I think we are. You are going to face the truth, come what may!

Knock on door. SOLOMON *jumps up in relief,* JUNE *opens door.* MAJID *confronts her in casual, Saturday afternoon attire.*

MAJID: May I come in?

SOLOMON (*from behind*): Of course, Majid. Come right in!

MAJID: Hope I'm not intruding?

SOLOMON: Great pleasure, old man. We were only talking. Have a seat. What can I offer you? Have a beer with me?

MAJID (*glancing at them both furtively and surprised by this excessive cordiality that is confined to* SOLOMON): No thanks, Solomon, I won't have anything really. My parents are in the car downstairs. I'm taking them out for a drive. But seeing your car I thought I would drop in and . . . (*shrugs*) well, I just wanted a word, really.

SOLOMON (*cordially*): Fire away, old man. There isn't anything you can say that she shouldn't know. She'd get to know it anyhow!

MAJID (*looking at them both, smiling slightly and then plunging into the matter*): I talked a lot at the G.D.M.'s party last night, Solomon.

SOLOMON: Ho, ho, you certainly did!

MAJID: But I hope you understood that I didn't really mean all I said.

SOLOMON (*astonished*): You didn't?

MAJID: Some of it maybe, but certainly not all.

SOLOMON (*not knowing what to say*): Well, that's all right, old man. We all say things at times. It certainly doesn't make any difference between us, I assure you.

MAJID (*eagerly*): Yes, that's what I want cleared. I know and we all know who the next G.M.'s going to be. You might be called this afternoon and offered formally. There's a meeting this morning so the decision has probably already been made. Let me congratulate you in advance and assure you of my personal loyalty.

JUNE: Ohhhhh!

SOLOMON (*glancing cock-surely at her*): Thank you, Majid. I know my friends now. I won't forget it, believe me. (MAJID *retreats to the door with a fixed smile, turns and is gone.*)

SOLOMON (*to* JUNE): You see, it's me!

JUNE: It definitely isn't!

SOLOMON (*staring at her*): What!

JUNE (*firmly now*): I said it definitely isn't.

SOLOMON (*shaking a finger at her*): If you carry on like this there will be trouble between us!

JUNE: Let's face it then and the sooner the better.

SOLOMON (*slumping into a chair*): What do you want from me?

JUNE: Firstly I want you to understand that you cannot under any circumstances accept this position when it is offered to you. It demands every ounce of your loyalty and energy. It needs a man like Mr Guru and if he were an African there would be no problem.

SOLOMON: You don't seem to understand that I am the only educated African engineer with any experience in the department.

JUNE: That doesn't make you the right man. Can you dedicate your life to this work? The country needs that at that level. It does not need men who will . . . will—

SOLOMON (*bitterly*): Go on say it! Men who will simply use the position to live comfortably.

JUNE: You wouldn't even do that much. Sooner or later you would be drawn back to your art. If you refuse to let it out it will fester and rot your inside till you are just a weakened, good-for-nothing man!

SOLOMON (*jumping up*): Stop! I don't want to hear any more.

JUNE: You must hear it all!

SOLOMON (*shouting*): Shut up, I said. You're a witch, a devil!

JUNE (*shouting*): And you're a liar, a cheat, a fake! You want a chair that doesn't fit you!

SOLOMON (*turning away in complete despair and clutching his hair*): Oh God, God, take this woman away. Shut up, I say!

JUNE (*suddenly quiet and watching him for a second before she speaks again, now quietly and with deadly effect*): You became an engineer because you couldn't stand the hard life you led in Europe trying to find yourself as an artist which is what God made you. You're afraid if you become a painter now you would be poor again. But that is nothing to fear. People will love and respect you when they understand what you are doing.

SOLOMON: People understand only money and force. In the position I am to get, I will have both. And that's what I want.

JUNE: That is not what you want and you know it. You're afraid of facing the future. You want comfort and the easy life now. But don't think people won't see through you. No one will respect you. You will be hated. And let me tell you that I will not remain either.

SOLOMON (*shaken*): What do you mean?

JUNE: Solomon, can't you understand? I love you for what you really are, not for this silly thing you're trying to become. If you were really an engineer at heart or even an ordinary man this would be the opportunity of a lifetime, but you are neither of these. You are an artist and it is only in that field that you can do any good in this world!

SOLOMON (*heavily*): If I refuse the offer to become G.M. will you be happy?

JUNE: No.

SOLOMON: No?

JUNE: You can't refuse that kind of position and then stay on in the department. It doesn't make sense. You must resign the service.

SOLOMON (*staring at her*): Give up my profession?

JUNE: You can't have two full-time professions.

SOLOMON: Have you gone mad? (*Banging the table with his fists.*) Absolutely mad, you woman!

JUNE (*calmly*): Not mad. Just sensible. I'm beginning to understand you for the first time. You have to make your choice one way or the other.

SOLOMON (*standing*): But this is mad, mad . . . mad! Look what you are asking me to throw up. A great position, a wonderful salary, fame even, just thrown at the whim of a woman! And why, for what, don't you think I'm human? Oh stop talking all this nonsense, June. I won't hear any more of it!

JUNE: Then your choice is made?

SOLOMON (*loftily*): It has to be, my country needs me.

JUNE: Well I don't and your country doesn't either. Goodbye!

SOLOMON: No, wait, stop, June!

JUNE (*hand on door*): Yes?

SOLOMON: But this is blackmail. You are asking me to commit suicide.

JUNE: I'm asking you to choose between right and wrong. (*Returning*) Solomon, I love you. Do you think I would ask you to do something that is not for your own good? Your choice can make you a free man or a slave for the rest of your life.

SOLOMON: But how can I . . . how can I? (*Pacing and sitting down abruptly with his head in his hands*) How can I throw all this away when it is being put in my hands. Do you know what poverty is? How can you? You have been fed and clothed all your life. You are a chief's daughter. How can you understand what it is to be a nobody, ignored by everyone because you have no money, no address, no decent clothes. . . . Just a . . . nobody!

JUNE (*softly*): You are thinking of Europe now, Solomon. This is our own country. Here I can work and earn for us both while you start again. No one will laugh at you. How can they? You are opening their eyes. Do you remember that day many years back in Cambridge when you took me out for a walk and we reached a field and you asked me to listen to the voice in the wind. With you beside me I heard it. And then when we returned you pointed out the colours all around us where I had never seen anything before but simple vegetation and trees. You changed my life that day.

SOLOMON: I don't know what to do now. (*Head in hands, starts sobbing.*)

JUNE (*kneels by his side with both hands on his head*): I will never leave you, Solomon.

SOLOMON *racked by sobs, subsiding. Knock on door.* JUNE *stands.* SOLOMON *leaves room.* JUNE *opens door.*

PREM: May I come in? (*There is a wrapped board under his arm.*)

JUNE: Good afternoon, Mr Guru. Please come in. Solomon will be out in a minute.

PREM: What a pleasant room. Did you furnish it for him?

JUNE: Well, I helped a little. But you know he is very good at colour himself.

PREM (*smiling*): I know.

SOLOMON (*returning from inside, recovered*): Good afternoon, sir, this is a pleasant surprise.

PREM (*chuckling*): Actually I suppose I should have warned you I was coming, but you have no telephone, it seems.

SOLOMON: I don't, that's quite right. But please do sit down. Can I offer you a beer?

PREM: Oh grand. Let's have one together. (*Sits, places parcel beside him against the wall.*)

JUNE: I'll bring it. (*Leaves room.*)

PREM (*turning to* SOLOMON): Perhaps you have an idea why I've come?

SOLOMON (*smiling*): I believe I have an idea.

PREM: The Minister wanted to have a word with you himself but he's tied up with another meeting this afternoon so I've come on his behalf, and my own, I should say.

Sighs . . . looks away for a second.

SOLOMON: Thank you, Mr Guru.

PREM (*silent, wondering how to begin.* JUNE *returns with two glasses of beer which she hands out. She makes to leave but* PREM *stops her*): I think you should sit with us my dear, this also concerns you. (SOLOMON *smiles again.*)

PREM (*continuing in a serious tone now*): Mr Wabera and I reached a decision last night as to who should be the next G.M. The decision is entirely that of the Minister, of course, but he consulted me as well.

SOLOMON: I understand, Mr Guru.

PREM: I'm glad you do, because the position of G.M. in the transport section is of importance to the country. It isn't just technical competence that is required. In fact at such levels technical competence, though desirable, is perhaps secondary. What is primary is dedication to duty and the allegiance of the staff to the new head.

SOLOMON (*nodding*): Quite right, sir.

PREM: But in a large public organization of this nature it also

demands the confidence of the man in the street for the head
of such an organization. Now we have in fact tried to take
all these various factors into account in making our choice.

SOLOMON: I understand, Mr Guru.

PREM: Dennis Githari was offered the post this morning. He has
accepted. I will, of course, give him the same loyalty that—

SOLOMON (*standing*): Dennis the new G.M.!

PREM (*quietly*): Yes.

SOLOMON: But . . . but I mean the man is uneducated!

PREM (*raising a finger*): Yet, very experienced and very reliable.

SOLOMON (*shaken*): Yes . . . of course. I don't have anything
against Dennis, but . . . but he isn't even a qualified engineer!

PREM: He will have a qualified staff under him. And he is
thoroughly familiar with the workings of the entire Transport Division. He has been in it longer than any of us.

SOLOMON (*turning away*): Yes . . . yes . . . I understand.

PREM (*standing and more soothing now*): It wasn't an easy decision
to make but I know we did right. (*Halts, then continues in a
different tone.*) There is another side to this as well. In choosing
Dennis for this post I hope we are releasing a new force into
the country.

SOLOMON (*turning back*): What do you mean?

PREM (*unwraps board and lays canvass against the wall*): It isn't
signed but whoever did that must continue with that work.
If it can be returned to me signed, it will be my most
treasured possession. (*Goes to door.*) Goodbye, Solomon.

SOLOMON: Goodbye sir.

JUNE: I will see you down, Mr Guru.

SOLOMON *alone on stage stands staring at the painting. Then his
hand goes out following a curve in it. Finally he smiles and goes up
to it as to an old friend.* JUNE *running back, stops at door, watching
him. Then picks up the pen from the table and hands it to him. He
kneels and signs.*

Curtain

The Exodus

TOM OMARA

Characters

NARRATOR
A GROUP OF CHILDREN
LABONGO*
GIPIR   } triplets
TIFUL†
LAWINO   Labongo's wife
OTEKA   Labongo's son

Time: Some centuries past
Place: East of the River Nile: present-day Acholiland

The NARRATOR sits among a group of children, either in front of the curtain, or among the audience.

NARRATOR: Tell me, my children, tell me tonight whether it is true that we today in Acholiland, whether we people east of this mighty river, this Nile, think of those living to the west or south of it as brothers.

1ST BOY: Why should we not be like brothers?

* Labongo is pronounced [laˈboŋo], that is with the 'ng' as in English 'sing'.

† This is the author's spelling, which derives from near the Sudan border. Elsewhere in Acholiland it would be 'Tipul' or 'Gipul'.

NARRATOR: Oh, you make me laugh. Does this mean you do not know the story of the beginning.

A GIRL: No, we don't.

2ND BOY: Tell us the story.

3RD BOY: The story of the beginning. Yes, I know it.

NARRATOR: Tell your brothers and sisters, then. Tell your generation. Your mothers should have told you this. My mother told me; and my mother's mother told her. That is how the story has lived on. Tell them, my son.

3RD BOY: Long, long ago, before anyone was born, God, the Moulder, the Nameless One, lowered to earth the First Man. Lwo was his name. Then the world was bare, like an egg's surface. There was nothing like buildings, cars, clothes, or even people except for this single man, Lwo. So that from Lwo spring all the people now alive, you and me. Isn't that right?

NARRATOR: Go ahead, boy. You know the story.

3RD BOY: Lwo had a grand-daughter who bore forth triplets. These brothers lived a life cursed by their own quarrels and jealousies among themselves. And one day there was such a big quarrel among them that they split up, and for ever after lived on opposite sides of the great river. I am right, aren't I, father?

NARRATOR: You are right. This quarrel was an important event.

3RD BOY: But we could put this story on the stage and act it, sir.

NARRATOR: So that these people would come back reclothed like spirits of our ancestors, do you mean?

3RD BOY: Yes.

NARRATOR: Then let us sing the song that tradition says must precede such a revelation.

They sing the Acholi song Canna. Our attention moves to the stage.

(NOTE: This play has frequently been performed without the above scene, but with a narrator speaking the following speech in its place:

NARRATOR: Long, long ago before anyone was born, God, the
Moulder, the Nameless One, lowered to earth the First Man.
Lwo was his name. Then the world was bare, like an egg's
surface. There was nothing like buildings, cars, clothes, or
even people, except for this single man, Lwo. So that from
Lwo spring all the people now alive, you and me. Lwo had
a grand-daughter who bore forth triplets. These brothers
lived a life cursed by their own quarrels and jealousies
among themselves. And one day there was such a big quarrel
among them that they split up, and for ever after lived on
opposite sides of the great river.)

First Movement

Dawn. A rough thatched hut has its door centre stage. Outside the
hut sits Lawino, a middle-aged woman dressed in animal skins or
bark-cloth. She is pounding grain-flour with mortar and pestle.
Thunder. A cock-crow.

LAWINO: Why does the cock crow so soon after thunder? This
is strange.
And yesternight the cricket chirruped at the
First cock-crow—a rare happening.
This is strange.

> GIPIR *bursts in in a great hurry. He is dressed in skins.*

GIPIR (*panting*): Where is a spear, a spear?
LAWINO: Why a spear at this early hour?
What beast can be hunted in this morning mist?
GIPIR: Where does Labongo keep his spears? Quick.
LAWINO (*still calm; stopping pounding*): What do you need it for?

GIPIR: Do not delay me.
 For look, a huge brown-tusked elephant
 Feeds in the millet field yonder.
 The entire plantation is fast turning brown,
 Like a cropless field.
LAWINO: Do something about it, then.
GIRPIR: I cannot do anything without a weapon.
 Give me any spear, now.
LAWINO: I have no ruling over the spear of Labongo.
 He is your brother, and I am nothing
 But a woman, a wife to him.

Impatient, GIPIR *enters the house, snatches a spear, comes out and dashes off with it.* LAWINO *shouts to him while he is in the hut*

Gipir, you should know your brother's temper,
A man so infinitely selfish and jealous,
Like a defeated bull.

(*Calling after him*)

Gipir! Gipir!
You dare take Labongo's ancestral spear—oh!

 TIFUL *dashes in, also dressed in skins.*

TIFUL: Gipir! Gipir! (*To* LABONGO) Gone!
 I thought I heard him talk hurriedly.
 I thought I saw someone like him bolt away, spear in hand.
LAWINO: Yes, you saw him.
TIFUL: Why, what was the spear for?
LAWINO (*calm but prompt*): What are spears for?
TIFUL: And whose was it?
LAWINO: Labongo's, my husband's. Why?
TIFUL: Does he not fear Labongo's anger?
 Does he not know Labongo's selfishness?
 Is he immune to his taunts?
LAWINO: What if he needed the spear then,
 And needed it desperately?

You are all brothers, born on the same day:

Why should there be strict possessions amongst yourselves?

TIFUL: But it is madness to take Labongo's possessions.

LAWINO: If you feel so strongly about it,

Why do you not make him spears yourself?

You are a blacksmith, aren't you?

Enter LABONGO, *with hoe and two spears, smaller than that* GIPIR *took. He has a calabash containing corn seeds in one hand. He puts these things down and sits on a log.*

LABONGO: Did you sleep well, brother?

TIFUL: I did. Did you also sleep well?

LABONGO: Yes, only I dreamt of rivers of spirits

Washing me away. I was washed to loneliness.

I was frightened, like a baby girl.

TIFUL: That was a bad dream.

I, too, dreamt of building a house in the wilderness,

Alone—unguarded by the Nameless one.

LABONGO: Both of us had evil dreams in the same night—
strange.

My wife told me I cried like a morning dove.

TIFUL (*to* LAWINO): Did you hear him cry?

LAWINO: Yes, he cried.

TIFUL (*changing the subject, points to hoe*): How was the ground?

LABONGO: Hard as a goat's horns.

It thundered this morning. Rain will come soon.

It will be a relief, for we are almost choked by drought.

TIFUL: I saw it rain at dawn this morning,

In that yonder valley, crammed with ghosts.

That was when it thundered here.

The sound of a horn is heard.

LABONGO: Sit yourself down.

Lawino, make ready some water for me for bathing.

She goes into the hut.

I have not seen Gipir for more than a day.

TIFUL: I thought I saw him.

LABONGO: When?

TIFUL: Just as I came along here.

OTEKA, *a boy of nine, scurries in.*

LABONGO: Yes, son, what is this hurrying for?

OTEKA: Oh father, there was an elephant in our field
And Gipir hurled a spear at it.

LABONGO: Where did it land?

TIFUL: Come, Labongo, let's go before it overpowers Gipir.

OTEKA: Don't go before I tell you more.

LABONGO: Were you afraid, son?

OTEKA: No. I am brave like you.
But when Gipir hurled the spear.
The great beast fell with a crash.
Then he took his horn and blew the tune of victory.

TIFUL: And is it dead there?

OTEKA: No, it is not.
It got up and fell, got up and fell,
Each time with a greater crash and Gipir was happier,
But when it got up the fifth time it ran away
With the spear in its body, and Gipir ran after it.
(*Softly, secretly*) But father, that was your ancestral spear.

LABONGO: My ancestral spear!

LAWINO *enters from the hut.*

TIFUL: And I thought I saw him run with it from here.

LABONGO (*very angry*): Woman, you must have given away my
spear.
I know you are going to deny it.
You are just a wife, and if you say no
I will kick you out like a rotten egg.

LAWINO: How you rage at me even before you know I did it.

LABONGO: Admit you gave my spear away.

LAWINO (*disgusted*): What if I did give it away?

LABONGO: Who told you to?

    Who told you to, you wretched woman?

    Tiful, do you not see the damage this woman has done to me?

    That spear was presented to me by my mother,

    And she made me vow never to let it out of these fingers.

TIFUL: Labongo, you are eaten up with anger.

LABONGO: Son, come here.

    Did you say the elephant actually ran away with my ancestral
      spear?

OTEKA: I know your spear well, father.

    And the spear I know is gone.

LABONGO: Now, Gipir, you hear for yourself.

    My spear is gone, gone for ever.

TIFUL: I will go and help Gipir chase this beast:

    An elephant is an animal that takes its revenge on men

    If quarrelled about. (*Exit.*)

LAWINO: Surely, and the elephant will avenge itself on Gipir

    If he is refused footing at home.

    What drives you so hard against a brother?

LABONGO: Shut that idle mouth, woman.

    Go indoors and pound your millet.

    Go before I am heated enough to beat you.

    Get out of here. (*She retires.*)

    (*To* OTEKA) And you, follow your mother.

    No, stay. I will talk with you.

    This cannot be.

    I will go to the field and recapture my spear myself.

    Get me my plumed head-dress, for I must go.

OTEKA: Yes, father. (*He starts to go out.*)

LABONGO: But stay a bit; I shall not go.

    Yes I *shall* go.

OTEKA (*confused*): Shall I fetch it, then?

LABONGO: No, do not.

    I am settled now. I shall not go.

    Gipir himself must bring my spear back.

C

If he does not,
I shall be enraged; I shall grow furious.
He will cry in my hands, helpless,
Like a mother about to give birth.

Enter TIFUL.

Have you found my treasure?
Where is Gipir?
Was the elephant there?

TIFUL: No, I could not trace its footsteps.
Even the dust that trailed behind it has vanished.
(*To* OTEKA) In which direction did it run?

OTEKA: It went towards where the sun rises.

TIFUL: Someone is panting like a dog after a pursuit.

Enter GIPIR.

Oh, Gipir!

LABONGO (*raging*): Where is my spear?
Who gave it to you?
How did you come to possess it?

GIPIR: You rain questions on me, brother.

LABONGO: You lose my spear and tell me I rain questions on
you!
Have you no shame?
You lost my spear out of sheer spite.
I knew you wanted to deprive me of my gift one day.
(*To* OTEKA) Go and call your mother here but do not return
yourself.

Exit OTEKA. LAWINO *enters*.

My ancestral spear, guard over all I possess, is gone.
Now, Tiful, look at that figure crouching
Clumsily, like a heap of potatoes dug by a mad boy.
That figure gave my spear away to this man out of sheer
vanity.

GIPIR: Brother, you rage.

Why do you refuse to listen to what happened?

LABONGO: I do not want to hear your story.

TIFUL: But, Labongo, you provoke danger to quarrel

About an animal of dread like an elephant.

GIPIR (*to* TIFUL): If he could wait till tomorrow

He would have his spear replaced.

LABONGO: Impossible, inconceivable.

I will take no replacement.

Who can replace a gift from another?

She herself received it from our great-grandfather, the first
man.

LAWINO: But Labongo, a replacement . . .

LABONGO: What? Replacement?

You have been lured into giving him my spear,

You woman, with rhythm.

GIPIR: I have not lain with her.

LABONGO: How do I know you did not?

What other act is so sweet as to move a woman

Into giving away a sacred possession?

LAWINO: You bring shame on me.

TIFUL: You malign your wife, brother.

You shame her before us all.

LABONGO: You can both go away if you find it shame.

You, Tiful, you depend on me so much

Yet you dare utter these words against me.

I hate you all.

GIPIR: Gipir, you treat me hard, as if we are not

Of the same lineage.

You rampage and curse us all.

I have borne all these things with coolness,

But now I am resolved to go and to come back

Only when I have retrieved that spear.

I shall follow the beast that strangled my good name

Even to the homestead of Death himself.

As long as I have my charms and my gods around me
I am content, like a thieving hyena on a dim-lit night.
(*Taking out his horn*) If you hear the sound of this horn,
Know that I am back with the spear.
If you hear nothing, I shall be dead.
Do not mourn.
Just beat the leopard drums for the ritual ceremony.
Beat them loud. Stay well. (*Exits quickly.*)

TIFUL: There goes a man deep and furious
As the river underground.

Second Movement

[*Time passes but the scene does not change.*]

LABONGO *is seated in front of the hut, sucking flour beer from a pot through a tube.* LAWINO *is on her knees boiling water.*

LAWINO: Yes, anybody could see that.
Anyone can observe that you have put a curse on your
   lineage.
You are the founder of man.
You can trace your descent from great grandfather Guly
And he was the first man on earth.

LABONGO: You have made me slow to anger.
In my time of high temper
I would have beaten the talking spirit out of you.
If my brother is dead, he is dead.

LAWINO: But you drove him to his death.
You drove him away from here.
You spurned him.
You accused him of playing rhythm with me.

Maybe though, dying, Gipir will be free of your wrath.
Perhaps that is how the Moulder planned it.
Who knows, he may be rotting in strange fields,
Eaten by crows and loathsome worms?

LABONGO: But how do you know he is dead?

LAWINO: If he is not, what has he been doing all this time?
For it is long since he went.
We have harvested three crops in that field since he left.
Truly, some dreadful fate must have befallen him,
Something absolute.

LABONGO: You speak of doom as if it were a thing avoidable.
If my great grandfather, the first man in this domain,
A man just moulded by God,
If he died,
Who am I not to die?
Who is Gipir not to meet his end?

LAWINO: But all could see it was your wrath
That drove him to his doom.
Do not run away from the truth.

LABONGO (*resigned*): Look, the fire goes out on the hearth.
Boil the water; I would like to put some more in this pot.
(*Looking at his hands*) My hands grow tough with digging.

LAWINO: The ground tills well, does it?

LABONGO: Yes, but the sorghum looks so lean,
As if the spirit of sunshine sucks water from it.

LAWINO: So long as some survives,
At least enough to brew some beer
For your brother's death ritual feast.

A horn is heard. Enter TIFUL.

TIFUL: Do you not hear a noise?

LABONGO: I do not hear anything. A knocking?

LAWINO: What does it sound like?

The horn sounds: '*Tu Tu Tu Tu*'.

TIFUL: There it goes again.

LABONGO: Yes, I heard it too.

TIFUL: I have been hearing it all this while.
It must be Gipir's horn, the lost one.

LAWINO: Without doubt that is him.
He told us the horn would be the signal for his return.

LABONGO: And that means my spear is back.

The horn sounds close.

TIFUL: There he comes, brightly plumed
Like weaver birds in the mating season.

GIPIR *enters, feathers on his head, with two spears, a horn and a calabash. They meet, embrace and shake hands vigorously.*

Oh brother!
The lost one, Gipir, is this actually you?

GIPIR: This is my destroyed state.

LAWINO (*kneeling*): We all give thanks for your home-coming.
Did the Nameless One guard you?
How was the wilderness?

LABONGO: Lawino, leave those questions. (*Shakes* GIPIR's *hand.*)
What gladness to have you home:
We were all so, so worried . . .

GIPIR (*handing him the spear, bitterly sarcastic*):
Here safe and sound the good spear comes home.
The wood is as oily as ever.
The metal is as shiny as ever.
The sharp end is sharp yet.
And the blunt end is blunt still.
Ho, I can breathe once more.

LABONGO (*smiling*): My ancestral spear indeed.
Tiful, this is overwhelming.
Give that calabash and your spear to Lawino.
Put them safely in the hut.
Get something for Gipir, for he must be hungry. (*Exit*
LAWINO.)

And for me, I must go to the river-bed.
I must build a shrine there.
I must take there a white goat for sacrifice.
The Moulder must know we rejoice in your home-coming.

GIPIR: Well, may you report things truly.

LABONGO: I shall be back soon. (*A pause.*)

Exit.

GIPIR: Is he out of hearing?

TIFUL: Yes, he is gone straight to the river-bed,
Reeling with extreme guilt like a dog
That steals simsim.

GIPIR: The whole place looks strange.
Labongo is strange now.
There is a restraint in everything here.
Even the wind blows with reserve.
Does there prevail any spirit unwelcome:
Does any ancestral spirit return to plague us all?

TIFUL: I know of no such spirit.

GIPIR: What then happened?

TIFUL: What happened?
Nothing, nothing at all.
Only now and again Labongo grew restless at your unreturn.
His pride is now deep hidden.
He has grown moodier every day.
He would sit on the verandah, shivering
Like a chicken beaten by rain.
To me it seemed his wife increased his sorrow,
For she always rebuked and reminded him.
It seemed he was so afraid within himself
That he one day called at my fire-place and asked
In a voice so frail:
'Tiful, what will God the Moulder say?
What will the spirit of our ancestors do,
Seeing that I have sent my brother to doom?'

GIPIR: And what did you say?

TIFUL: I frowned and yawned, that's all.
What can a man say, a man as feeble as I?
If I said anything he disliked, who could defend me?
What spirit can stand up for a feeble man? None.

GIPIR: No, Tiful, no.
You fool yourself; you belittle yourself.
You could stand up against Labongo.
If his temper overwhelmed him, you could run amok too,
And that would quiet him.

TIFUL: And you, what happened to you?
You have been away so long.

LAWINO *enters and sits.*

GIPIR: Lawino, you are not going to tell all that I say
To Labongo? For that would reek blood.

LAWINO: Gipir, you should trust me more than that.

TIFUL: What happened? How was the wilderness?

GIPIR: We have been brought up in the wilderness.
Our mother reared us in the forest wilderness.
But the forest, the wilderness I met was different.
There dwelt beasts of every tribe.
Snakes venomous, big-headed vipers, night adders,
Lions, buffaloes, wildebeests, gazelles,
Rhinoceroses with horns
That would make the skin of a cow itch in fear and wonder.
A beast, a sadist by nature, a beast . . .

LAWINO: Oh, unlucky man.

TIFUL: How did you survive all these things?

GIPIR: I survived because I went always forward.
I was bent, I was determined to find the spear.
I followed the footprints of the elephant.
But after a few days I grew famished.
I could not stomach the fruits and roots of the wilderness.

But one day, in despair, I decided to eat them:
I couldn't have survived long without them
For my whole body had grown a skeleton.
For days I suffered with cold;
I was beaten by rain and hailstones
Without even a cave to shelter me.
My fingers and toes grew numb at times.
But one day something most strange happened to me.
Maybe I was half asleep and half awake;
Maybe I was completely asleep.
Somehow I sensed something speak to me within myself.
Then suddenly I saw a dismal figure, big as an elephant.
It quickly turned into an old, old woman.
Then she led me to her house—
A horror-haunted place, bleak and without sun.

TIFUL: Then were you frightened?

GIPIR: How could I even know I was frightened?
I was numb, maybe with fright.
She took me to a room where there were
Many, many spears,
Spears of different forms.
Then suddenly she burst out talking: I cowered.
And she said: 'Take your spear from that row.
But if you hurl a spear at an elephant again,
You shall be for ever haunted by elephants.'
It was then that I realized
She was the spirit of an elephant dressed as a woman,
For she went on: 'Swear you'll not touch our race again.'
And I swore.
Then she gave me a bead white as a baby's tooth
To wear as a guard against forest beasts.
And the old woman of the forest went on:
'Gipir, you must away from this forest,
For it is a realm of departed spirits,
Spirits dejected, spirits offended and spirits revengeful.'

And so I walked back, though it was days and days
Before I was out of the forest.

LAWINO: And where is that bead?

GIPIR: It is in the calabash you took into the hut.

LAWINO: Oh, poor man, you bore all these hardships:
You must be so hardened.

TIFUL: Did the elephant woman say anything
About Labongo's anger?

GIPIR: Yes: that Labongo's spite against me was very sharp.

LAWINO: The spite overawes him now. (OTEKA *enters from hut*.)
Go away. Go back.
You dare come to talk among older people!

OTEKA: But listen, mother.

LAWINO: What is it I have to listen to right now. (*Cry of baby*.)

OTEKA: The child has swallowed a white stone.

LAWINO: Where were you looking when it did so?
Let me go. (*Enters hut followed by* OTEKA.)

GIPIR: Tiful, perhaps that is my sacred bead,
That given me by the old woman,
For it is white.

TIFUL: This is another problem. (*Cry of baby. Enter* LABONGO.)

LABONGO: All is over:
The goat of sacrifice lies dead in the shrine,
A gift to the Moulder. (*Cry of baby*.)
What is that cry for?

TIFUL: Something snatches your house into disorder. (*Cry of baby*.)

LABONGO: I must find out. I must. (*Enters hut. Pause. Cry of baby*.)

GIPIR: My precious bead is just as valuable
As Labongo's ancestral spear.

TIFUL: Do not ask for as hard a return
As he did from you;
For someone seeing us now would think
We are half-brothers whose different mothers

Show one another the cat's jealousy of a dog,
And not brothers born and nurtured
By the same woman.
Refrain from stern action.

GIPIR: I cannot forget my suffering so soon.

TIFUL: What will you do then if the child
Cannot give up the bead?

GIPIR: Do not ask what I shall do.
Ask Labongo.
When I lost his spear, did he care to find it himself?
I cannot forget the pains I endured so soon. (*Anguished
cry.*)

TIFUL: That sharp cry.
I fear they are trying to force it out of the child.

Enter LABONGO.

LABONGO: Gipir, we have tried to pluck the bead out of the
child;
But, as if the act is cursed, we have failed.
We have given it herbs, but nothing happens,
As if the herbs have suddenly
Become impotent:
Even the tortoise's scales could not help.

GIPIR: Labongo, what I want is my bead.
I cannot forget my suffering so soon.

LABONGO: You know a child is a thing preciousest.
We cannot get the bead out without having
To cut open the child.
Therefore, brother, I implore you, accept a replacement.

GIPIR: Labongo, what do you think I am made of?
Do you think I can easily forget your wrath?
Did you ever care into what hazards you spurned me
When you refused to accept another spear?
You bellowed at me, and accused me
Of playing rhythm with your wife, as if I were ...

As if I were a duckling and you a chicken,
And not a brother of the same blood,
As if I had most grossly wronged' you before.
You did not know I would have my turn for revenge.

LABONGO: Gipir, you forget this is my home.
Do not brawl over me thus; (*He draws out a knife.*)
For my child will I cut open
With this knife, to get that evil bead.

TIFUL: Labongo, you take matters with a child's hatred.

LABONGO: You coward, you weakling,
A man unable to hurl a spear even at a hare,
How do you come to challenge me?

TIFUL: Labongo, you talk like an old witch.
What kind of braveness is that
Which makes you so slight-tempered?
You are jealous
Yet you call yourself strong.
What sort of strength is that
Which makes you strong for the wrong things?

LABONGO (*running at* TIFUL *with knife, held back by* GIPIR):
You tell me that in my own home?
You make me seethe with anger.
Will you laugh at my strength now?

TIFUL: Come, Gipir, rescue me. Hold him.

GIPIR (*grasping* LABONGO's *free hand*): Stop it, man.

LABONGO: Let my hand go.
You have saved that coward.
Let free my hand.
I will go and get your bead. (*Wrenches himself free: enters the hut. Pause.*)

GIPIR: But the child he is about to pierce through
Is innocent like a lamb.
I'll prevent the act. (*Encounters* OTEKA *at hut door.*)

The cry of a child.

OTEKA: Oh help, help, Gipir.
My father is killing our child.

LAWINO rushes in; throws herself on GIPIR, weeping.

LAWINO: Help, Gipir, quick.
My husband is cutting open the child.
Stop him if you're a man.
Do it if you are a man.
GIPIR: Let free my hands, then.
Let free my hands. (*He pulls free.*)

Enter LABONGO with blood-stained knife. He carries the bead.

LAWINO: Oh, he is finished.
Oh he, my child!
My child, my child . . . (*Her voice trails off.*)
LABONGO: Now you can get your prized thing. (*He throws down the bead.*)
Take it. (GIPIR *takes the bead:* LABONGO *throws down the knife.*)
Hold one spear.
GIPIR: I hold it: but not for a fight.
LABONGO: Nay, not for a fight,
But to swear.
GIPIR: To swear indeed.

LABONGO and GIPIR cross their spears ceremonially.

LABONGO: Hold it high.
Let its blade shimmer with a glow;
And we must swear,
Swear to part company henceforth.
GIPIR: We must swear never to meet again.
LABONGO: Never to meet again as brothers . . .
GIPIR: But as enemies on the battlefield.
LABONGO: And not to spare one another.
And as for dwelling place,

I on the east bank of the River Nile
Will settle.

GIPIR: To let the crushing river divide us,
I to the west of the river
Will build a home.

LABONGO: To You, the Moulder,

GIPIR: To You, the Nameless One,

LABONGO: To you, the ancestral spirits,

LABONGO and GIPIR (*together*): We take this vow,

GIPIR: And swear to keep it with an equal mind.

LAWINO *is weeping*; OTEKA *leans against her, also crying.* LABONGO *and* GIPIR *swing round simultaneously, back to back, their spears rasping apart, and exit in opposite directions.* LAWINO *and* OTEKA *follow* LABONGO. TIFUL, *alone, creeps forward fearfully, picks up the blood-stained knife, slowly looks after* LABONGO *and* GIPIR *in turn, and exits into the hut as the play ends.*

Of Malice and Men

GANESH BAGCHI

Characters

SONA SEN
SUDHIN SORCAR
MICHAEL KNIGHT

Place: The sitting-room of KNIGHT'S *house in a Commonwealth country: Bilaspore*

Time: A month after Independence.

> MICHAEL KNIGHT, *a bachelor, about twenty-five years old, is packing. He is wearing khaki drill trousers and a coloured shirt. He looks rather dishevelled. His sitting-room looks even more dishevelled with packing boxes all over the place, packing boxes of different sizes and shapes, and books, clothes, pictures, shoes, etc., lying about in the most unlikely places. There is little or no furniture.*
>
> MICHAEL KNIGHT *is packing, and everybody can hear it. At the opening of the curtain all that anybody can hear is the loud din of hammer on the packing boxes. Quite obviously,* MR KNIGHT *is getting a lot of satisfaction out of driving nails into his packing boxes. There is a knock on the door, soft at first, then becoming very loud.*

MICHAEL: Go away, there's nobody at home. (*He gets on with his hammering. The door opens and in comes* SONA.)
SONA (*looking round and ignoring* MICHAEL): So there's nobody at home, is there? How odd, how very odd.

MICHAEL: What do you want?

SONA: Nothing, my darling. I've merely come to see, once again, your fair face, and your noble upright figure before you finally depart to find your place and fulfil God's purpose in obscure Tunbridge Wells.

MICHAEL: Go away, Sona, I'm busy.

SONA: What's the matter with you, Michael?

MICHAEL: I'm not going to explain. Why shouldn't I be rude if I want to? Just because your country has got its independence, it doesn't mean we have lost ours. We've gone on being polite to each other in our lovely, lovely, plural society and hidden all our malice and frustration behind our public face. Where has it got us?

SONA: I don't want you to do anything out of bitterness, Michael. You've always said you liked it here. Why do you all want to leave the boat now as if there's a fire in the engine room?

MICHAEL: I don't know. Anyway, I've convinced myself I don't like it here any more.

SONA: What will you do? You can't do much virus-research in Tunbridge Wells, can you?

MICHAEL: There's room for all in our affluent society. I'll do my work, and on Sundays I'll have tea with Aunt Emily. I'll get back to my T.V. by the fire-place and the Sunday morning newspapers; to grey skies, the cold, the drizzle and the damp; to drab English architecture, provincial art and provincial tarts; to meetings of young conservatives and fish and chips.

SONA: That doesn't sound very exciting, does it?

MICHAEL: I know it doesn't, but that's where lie my roots.

SONA: That's fascinating, isn't it? You come here and get our values all mixed up. We take you seriously when you talk of one world and cultural cross-currents and the role of people like you and me. And then, suddenly, someone cries fire, and before you can say knife, you're ready to run back to your roots. Why?

MICHAEL: Because there's no other way, because we always grab what we can get today and never think of tomorrow. And when tomorrow comes, there's only one way left—to get out.

SONA: I don't want you to go, Michael, feeling hurt and bitter.

MICHAEL: Don't worry, Sona. It'll be all right. You'll settle down in Bilaspore, and I'll settle down in Tunbridge Wells. You'll marry Sudhin, and I'll marry someone called Mary or Jane, and before the year is out we'll have put each other on our respective lists for Christmas cards and come to terms with ourselves.

SONA: You needn't worry about me, Michael. Now that you're going, I don't want you to worry, do you understand? That's one insult you'll spare me, won't you?

MICHAEL: There's nothing time won't heal.

SONA: God, how profound can you get! The wisdom of the English is proverbial. 'There's nothing time won't heal.' 'The time's come, my darling, so let's smile and say "Goodbye".' If you dare say anything like that to me again, I'll have no doubt at all that you and Aunt Emilda of Tunbridge Wells deserve each other.

MICHAEL: Actually, my aunt is called Emily, not Emilda.

SONA: Does it matter?

MICHAEL: Actually, I suspect, Aunt Emily has got rather used to her name over the last fifty years and might not like the change.

SONA: I don't like changes either. If I don't mind being forsaken by my lover at the tender age of twenty-four, your illustrious aunt shouldn't mind changing her name at fifty, should she?

MICHAEL: Actually you're twenty-six, two years older than I am, aren't you?

SONA: Actually I was being carried away by my emotion.

MICHAEL: That's one thing we must not do: be carried away by emotion.

SONA: Does Aunt Emilda also believe in facts?

MICHAEL: Actually, Aunt Emily is a very factual old spinster who agitates regularly for banning the bomb for the preservation of the human race. But can't we get away from the subject of Aunt Emily?

SONA: What's the use? I don't for a moment believe that this wild adventurer who came to benighted Bilaspore to preach the gospel of one world can really keep away from the blessings of his affluent society, and the symbol of security which is Aunt Emily.

MICHAEL: What I don't understand is why you should come and insist on discussing Aunt Emily at such length, just when I was quietly getting on with my packing.

SONA: 'Quietly' did you say? I live five blocks away and because of the din you were making, I could not hear myself think.

MICHAEL: You should thank me for that, don't you think? I'm of the opinion that a Hindu woman is singularly ill-equipped to sort out what a Hindu woman thinks.

SONA: Thanks. I find you're becoming quite an expert on the subject of Hindu women.

MICHAEL: Why not? I became a soccer blue at Cambridge because I could speak Sanskrit.

SONA: Why Sanskrit?

MICHAEL: I've always had a taste for the exotic.

SONA: You a soccer blue because of your Sanskrit, and I a scarlet woman because of my association with you. Colourful paradox all this, don't you think?

MICHAEL: In our case, it's more the paradox of colour, I'm afraid.

SONA: Simple as that?

MICHAEL: I don't care whether it's simple or not, I'm going to make it simple. I'm going to be what's considered to be typical of my race: good, virtuous, stolid, respectable, complete with bowler hat and rolled-up umbrella, in every detail the popular image, the delight of Tunbridge Wells, one of the pillars of our provincial society . . .

SONA: And the apple of Aunt Emily's eye.

MICHAEL: Sona, there is something you want to tell me. What is it? All right. You don't want to ask me what you came to ask me. You want to know why I'm going away, how I can go away if I love you.

SONA: It does seem very odd.

MICHAEL: I'm going because suddenly everybody's going, and I've a feeling that everybody's waiting for me to go. I'm convinced this is what I've always wanted to do.

SONA: Suppose you said, 'I'm not going. I'm digging my heels in because I belong here.'

MICHAEL: That's no good at all, Sona. One in ten thousand might understand what I meant, but most people would be suspicious of something terribly subtle and under-hand. To my colleagues in the office, I'm a vacancy for which they're going to apply; to people like Sudhin, I'm a reminder of their humiliation. And nothing will change that attitude of mind, nothing at all, and the baby must go with the bathwater.

SONA: I still don't understand what all this fuss is about. I believe people can live together just by being together and by not harking back to their roots. I belong here, because I happen to be here. But if your thoughts and actions are manipulated by some kind of remote control from across the seas, then it's another matter.

MICHAEL: But that's how it's always worked, and that's how it's going to work. I want to go, I will not live with tension and suspicion. I'm hurt and angry because we've all been so stupid. We've all mouthed our Commonwealth ideology all these days, but when we're reduced to tin-tacks we find that what binds us together is political expediency and cash nexus, and there's very little that's really human between us. Mind you, I'm not blaming Sudhin and his kind. I know my own people only too well to want to justify their ways to you or to God. I don't want to think or feel or argue about anything any more. I just want to go.

SONA: Whichever way I turn, people just say, 'I just want to go.'

MICHAEL: And some people are jolly glad it's that way.

SONA: I am not glad that you're going, but maybe it's got to work out this way. You can go on putting your beastly nails into your beastly packing boxes. Goodbye, Michael.

MICHAEL: Goodbye, Sona.

As he says goodbye, MICHAEL *moves towards* SONA. *There's a knock on the door.* MICHAEL *opens the door as* SONA *hides behind a packing box.* SUDHIN *is about thirty-four. He looks perturbed.*

SUDHIN: Is Sona here, Mr Knight?

MICHAEL: Good evening, Mr Sircar.

SUDHIN: Good evening, Mr Knight. Is Sona here?

MICHAEL (*with a straight face*): No, Mr Sircar. Sona isn't here.

SUDHIN: Thank you, Mr Knight. Goodnight. (SUDHIN *goes out.*)

SONA (*emerging from behind the packing box*): You lied, Mr Knight.

MICHAEL: I lied to protect you.

SONA: I didn't ask for your protection.

MICHAEL (*angrily*): All right. I'll call him back. (MICHAEL *calls out.*) 'Mr Sircar, Mr Sircar.'

Enter SUDHIN.
SONA *has hidden behind the packing box.*

MICHAEL: I'm sorry, Mr Sircar. I lied to you about Sona. The truth is I know where Sona is but I'm not going to tell you.

SUDHIN: Thank you very much, Mr Knight. Goodbye.

SONA (*emerging from behind the packing box*): Well, Sudhin, Michael needn't tell you where I am. I'm here.

SUDHIN: So you are. But I don't think you're going to be here much longer, because you're coming with me.

SONA: Why?

SUDHIN: Because your father is worried. He is waiting for you. He's asked me to bring you home.

SONA: My father has told me many things in his time but I haven't taken the slightest notice of them.

SUDHIN: But this time you are going to, and that's why I'm here.

MICHAEL: Are you suggesting Mr Sircar, that you are going to take her away from here by force?

SONA: This is tribal warfare, Michael. You keep out of this.

MICHAEL: I'll keep out of this only as long as I can.

SUDHIN: Aren't you satisfied with messing up our national life, Mr Knight, that you want to mess up the lives of trusting individuals like Sona?

SONA: I'm quite capable of looking after myself, Mr Sircar. You needn't worry. In any case Mr Knight has decided that he should go back to his roots and I to mine, so there's no problem.

SUDHIN: It's a very wise decision.

MICHAEL: I haven't asked for your comments or advice, have I?

SUDHIN: It's been your privilege to be our self-appointed friend, philosopher and guide all these years. Why should you mind?

MICHAEL: We don't want that privilege any more. We're going.

SUDHIN: That's not why you're going. The moment you find others in your position of privilege or making your mistakes, you shriek with impatience.

MICHAEL: I know exactly what you're going to say. 'The British are arrogant, superior, selfish, short-sighted, hypocritical, parochial' etc., etc. But take India, for example.

SUDHIN: Please do not take India for example.

MICHAEL: Why not?

SUDHIN: You couldn't choose a worse example.

SONA: Michael, can you suggest something I can do while you two get on with your friendly conversation?

MICHAEL: Go home and go to bed.

SUDHIN: I'll come.

SONA: Don't be silly. I don't want to go home or go to bed.

MICHAEL: Then sit down and read a book or get on with the packing or something.

SONA *takes up a hammer and starts nailing up a packing box.*

SUDHIN: Stop that, for goodness sake. We can't talk if you make that noise.

SONA: I'm making a more pleasant noise than you are.

MICHAEL: A few unpleasant noises don't do anybody any harm anyhow. Mr Sircar, I want you to tell me with complete honesty whether you deny that we were ever inspired by a few great ideals?

SUDHIN: Maybe you were, but your small men have made short work of your great ideals.

MICHAEL: I see. Would you also deny that we managed to give your country a sense of unity and direction, whatever our faults?

SUDHIN: Unity did you say?

MICHAEL: Yes, I said 'Unity'. Who gave you common law and justice, a common language, a unified system of administration, order and organization, roads and buildings, health services and education, civilized ways of living and thinking, and a link with the world outside?

SUDHIN: I'll tell you what I think. I think you've been ingenious, but not honest. You've organized your exploitation in the manner and through methods with which you're familiar. You've created a hierarchy of civil servants and privileged classes of local people to buttress your own system which you've inflicted on us. And what you've given, you've given from outside, with arrogance, not with love. How do you account for the fact that wherever you've gone, you've formed an alliance with the reactionary elements of the country and remained always, absolutely always, the eternal outsider?

MICHAEL: The trouble with you is that you refuse to see that things are changing, things have changed. You, Mr Sircar, still talk like the patriots of the thirties. Why do you ask me questions when you're so confident that you know all the answers?

SONA: I will not let this go on. I'm fed up with men and their

malice. What does it matter what the British didn't do and
the Indian didn't deserve and the Africans haven't got? You
men all act from built-in prejudices and fear of each other,
not from honesty of intellect or purity of emotion, which, as
far as I am concerned, are the same thing. So you face each
other like a couple of prizefighters and go on bandying
words till the cows come home. But do you ever try to know
each other, give each other a chance?

SUDHIN: You tried desperately hard to know and understand
Mr Knight. But did you get anywhere, did you? Look at all
the packing boxes (*laughs cynically*). This is called strategic
withdrawal—something his nation learned at the last war.
When you can't get the best of both worlds, get out. That's
an old English proverb.

SONA: You want Michael to stay so that, at the slightest opportunity, you can tell him that he doesn't belong here, make
him feel that he's here on sufferance, accuse him of being a
mercenary masquerading as a do-gooding idealist?

SUDHIN: Can you blame anybody if he accuses the British of a
little hypocrisy? Look at their history. Haven't they clung to
individual liberty in their own country? Isn't it the one thing
they have always refused to exchange for anything else? Yet,
how is it that it is the one thing they have stubbornly refused
to concede whenever they have come out of their country?

MICHAEL: Look, Mr Sircar, I'm sick of this stuff. This is the
kind of thing that every schoolboy nationalist has been saying
for years. I know it all.

SUDHIN: There are schoolboys, Mr Knight, who know their
books backwards but learn nothing from them.

MICHAEL: There are books, Mr Sircar, which make more sense
when read backwards.

SONA: And there are people, gentlemen, who sound more and
more angry and ignorant as they proceed with their argument.

MICHAEL: Please, Sona. I haven't finished with Mr Sircar yet.

SUDHIN: And I've not finished with Mr Knight either.

SONA: I don't care whether you've finished with each other or not, I have finished with both of you. You're a bore and Sudhin's a bore, and men generally are a bore. I hate them all.

MICHAEL: All right, get thee to a nunnery or something, but leave us alone.

SONA: You're very rude. (*She walks towards the door, but then stops and sits down on a chair, picks up a book and begins to read.*)

MICHAEL: Yes, Mr Sircar.

SONA (*lifting her head from the book*): You mean 'No, Mr Sircar', don't you? You're not going to cut the ground from under his feet by agreeing with him, are you?

MICHAEL: No, Sona. I was not agreeing with him. I was saying, 'Yes, Mr Sircar, I'm ready and you can shoot your lines about colonialism, imperialism and the British.'

SUDHIN: Actually, it's your turn now, Mr Knight.

MICHAEL: Don't be too fair. It might become a habit.

SUDHIN: Don't worry, Mr Knight. I do that from time to time just for variety.

SONA (*looking up from her book*): Enjoy your freedom to be fair while you can. You may not even have the freedom to be fair for very long.

SUDHIN: What do you know of fairness, Sona? Because you read a little English at the University and filled up your head with romantic notions about the English, you think every English-man you meet is a Burke, a Cobbett, a Lawrence, or Henry James.

SONA: Henry James was American, not English.

MICHAEL: That's not the point.

SUDHIN: I was talking about fairness. I was saying that people like Sona talk a lot of nonsense about fairness when they haven't the slightest notion of what it means. I'm convinced there can't be any question of fairness between Mr Knight and me, only the question of survival.

MICHAEL: People like you, Mr Sircar, bring out the worst in me with your political, economic jargon. What I've always believed is that there are everywhere in this world, a group of people who are rootless because they do not accept loyalties, because they can put down their roots anywhere provided they're allowed to have a sense of belonging. I've lived here so long, I've loved Bilaspore so much, that I feel I belong here. Who are you to tell me; I don't? When I went away to England for a few years, I enjoyed my life at the University but I missed the clear blue sky of Bilaspore and my friends here. I thought of Bilaspore as my home and I counted the days, patiently waiting to come back here. Wherever I saw signs of a new kind of agressive nationalism among my people, I protested. Everybody must have the right to choose his country, I said. But now Mr Sircar says this is not going to work. I want to tell you, Mr Sircar, that whether I belong here or not is something I decide and you have no right to tell me where I belong, do you understand? I know your feelings and attitudes towards me, but I'd like to point out to you, Mr Sircar, that I'm not an investment, but an individual, and would like to be treated as one.

SONA: If you want to be treated as an individual, Mr Knight, why don't you behave like one? You're doing exactly what everybody else is doing. Yet you want to be treated as an individual! You're going away because you're fed up with the stupidity of me and people like me. But how are you going to escape from the stupidity of the people in your country?

MICHAEL: I'm not responsible for the stupidity of people here or anywhere else. All I know is that it's on account of people like you that my participation in the life of the people here is suspect, and I do not like it.

SUDHIN: In the circumstances, I think you've made the wisest decision. If you go away, there's no problem.

SONA: You seem to be in a bit of a hurry to get rid of Michael, don't you, Sudhin?

SUDHIN: I don't see what he loses by going away. He goes back to his roots and we stay with ours. What's more, the Government is going to compensate Mr Knight for the loss of property and loss of face.

MICHAEL: God! How you people talk! What kind of arrogance is it to think that you can take away a man's land, his job, his love, his sense of identification with a country where, in many cases, he has grown up and his children have grown up, not knowing any other country, and compensate him for all this with a sum of money?

SUDHIN: I know many of your countrymen whose one concern has been how much money they're getting.

MICHAEL: Let's stick to the subject, shall we? And the subject is me, not my countrymen.

SUDHIN: How can I isolate you from your countrymen?

SONA: If I may say so, you can't, Sudhin, because you aren't very intelligent, so you lump them all together. The moment you begin to accept people as individuals, who don't fall into the pattern of your thinking, you get really worried, don't you?

SUDHIN: The individual, my dear Sona, has been as dead as the dodo for a long time. Who is your new individual? The organization man? The angry young man? The teddy boy and the beatnik? They're all so predictable! Couldn't you have written down exactly how people were going to react to Bilaspore's Independence? There's only one kind of response today—the group response: only, there are individual forms of rationalization. Why blame me? I generalize because individual variations are rare, I predict because people are so frighteningly predictable.

MICHAEL: Would you say, Mr Sircar, that your reactions are in any way unusual?

SUDHIN: There's a time for subtleties and a time for brute realities. I must tell you the obvious truth because I can't afford to be misunderstood.

SONA: So that's a concession you make for less intelligent people than yourself?

MICHAEL: Our misunderstanding started a long time ago, and the more we've lived together, the less we've understood each other. Now whether we stay together, or stay apart it's all one.

SONA: In that case, why bother to go?

SUDHIN: Mr Knight must go. It's the path laid out by history.

MICHAEL: You know, Mr Sircar, the more you want me to go, the more I want to stay.

SUDHIN: You know, Mr. Knight, the more you stay, the more you'll want to go away.

SONA: That sounds like a threat to me. Are you suggesting that . . .

SUDHIN: I'm not suggesting anything. I'm merely stating what I believe is a fact.

MICHAEL: You're really making it difficult for me to decide now. I'd absolutely made up my mind to go but now . . .

SUDHIN: He who walks firmly to his goal is a man, Mr Knight.

SONA: You insist that Mr Knight walks firmly to Tunbridge Wells?

SUDHIN: Yes, I do.

SONA: What do you think of that, Michael?

MICHAEL: The fact that it might please Mr Sircar if I went away is beginning to bother me a little.

SUDHIN: And it has always bothered me a great deal when you and your people have told us 'Take this and take that and be grateful, for you have nothing to give back in return.' No human relationship is possible in that kind of situation, and I resent it. As long as you stay on here wanting to help us as outsiders, you'll make me feel inferior, and I don't like that feeling.

SONA: Whether you feel inferior or not is your business, it isn't a national issue!

SUDHIN: Nonsense! History makes me feel inferior, my social

and political status makes me feel inferior. When the price of cotton and coffee invariably goes down and the price of cars invariably goes up, I feel inferior. It's Mr Knight's privileged function to make me feel inferior. For the last sixty years, the whole machinery of government has been geared to the purpose of making me feel inferior. If Mr Knight feels superior to me, it's because history has been on his side.

MICHAEL: You're crying havoc, Mr Sircar, merely because you want your voice to be heard above mine. But your turn will come, and God help you if you haven't learnt anything from our mistakes.

SUDHIN: A few like you, Mr Knight, will desperately flap their arms so that they don't fall off the moral pedestal. But they'll fall, they have fallen. There'll be no more pedestals, only the Common Market, and second-class citizens like Sona and me in your country. But here in Bilaspore, let's live with self-respect, Mr Knight. Sona, I want you to understand that Mr Knight's love for you is not simple and human, it's the institutional pity of the self-conscious soggy liberal with a dash of sex and the stink of guilt. If you've any self-respect . . .

SONA: Shut up, Sudhin, and don't be impertinent. If you haven't convinced me before, you won't convince me now. Why do you men always pretend to be greater than you are? Why do you snarl at his system, when you're both the victims of the same organized stupidity which holds out no other promise except the promise of self-destruction? If you only realized this, you would not wear yourselves out in this manner. Who are you fighting each other for? For people to whom war is a game of chess, for a system that swamps all humanity out of us? We're victims, Sudhin, you and me and Michael, not heroes, and the only interest of this *system* is to sell to us the idea that nations and races live by throttling each other. Don't you realize that our only way is to stick together as individuals and fight this system which insults, instead of fighting each other?

SUDHIN: I don't see how we three can stick together. The ideal of living together is not Mr Knight's ideal and we've seen that in our country. Let's not live together, let Mr Knight go, let's see what we can do by living on our own. He's given up, he's going away, and Sona, you've known me much longer than you've known him. Sona, can't we do something now with our lives, you and me together?

SONA: No, Sudhin, you're too full of yourself, too arrogant and aggressive to love anyone. I don't understand your language.

SUDHIN: But, can't you see it's because of the way you threw me aside that I'm what I am? Before Mr Knight came between you and me, things were different. If you care for me just a little, Sona, it's going to be different.

SONA: Now it's no use at all, Sudhin. I can't turn back. Michael will go, and you'll hate me for always, but what can I do? I'll have to wait, through the dreariness and the drought, for the new rain.

SUDHIN: All right, Sona. I've nothing more to say. Only, look out, Sona. When everything is lost, when all your love and tenderness for Mr Knight is lost in the indiscriminable darkness of race and hate, don't come to me. You're naïve, you're too full of trust to know how vicious this game is. But I'll leave you to your destiny. Goodbye. (*Exit* SUDHIN.)

SONA *doesn't say anything. She stands quite still for a few moments, then speaks quietly and with conviction.*

SONA: I'm not afraid. If you want to go, Michael, you must go and not look back.

MICHAEL: As I think of going away, I feel frightened by the spectre of grey desolation which spreads before me to the end of the horizon. But as the sun of our imperial glory goes down, I can see the shadows of our past lengthen and fall on the present, separating you from me, me from Sudhin. Now

Sudhin and his boys will get together and try to wipe out the past, fight the shadows, make the same mistakes we've made and the same voyage to the empty land of more power and more money. I can see it all happening.

SONA: If you accept what Sudhin has said, that the finger of history points in the direction of Tunbridge Wells, I've nothing more to say. I'll go.

MICHAEL: I can't let you go alone.

SONA: Please don't try to protect me. I can walk alone. We must all walk alone at night to conquer our fear of darkness. Goodbye.

MICHAEL: Don't go yet. Listen to me, Sona. I don't know what's right and what's wrong, I feel confused and helpless. But I'm sure it's wrong to let silly notions of race and politics come between one individual and another. I will not believe that I can ever let any kind of group-loyalty—national, political or religious—undermine our personal human relationship. It's because we've made our systems with machines, not with the mellow hands of human beings, that things have fallen apart, and our systems have sucked life out of us. This needn't go on, this mustn't go on, Sona, and we can do something about it. Will you help me, Sona? It's no use my running away, because, for breaking out of this confusion, for the illumination of my emptiness, I need your love, Sona, more than anything else in the world. Will you give it to me?

SONA: Don't ask me any questions, Michael, for, if you do, you must find the answers. My love has no will and no words, no thinking, no conscious feeling, only movement, or the awareness of a wordless, will-less movement of my entire being towards the radiant centre of light which is you, and, suddenly there is no 'you' and no 'me' but only oneness into which everything has melted.

They embrace as the Curtain falls.

The Secret

AUGUSTINE BUKENYA

Characters

NAKIBINGE   The king
NATTU ⎫
NDAGIRE ⎬ his sisters
NANNONO   One of his wives
MPISI   A warrior
KAGALI ⎫
GUNJU ⎬ Officers
JITA ⎭
WARRIORS, EXECUTIONERS, PRISONERS, etc.

A horn sounds five times, and the curtain rises on the King's tent in the bush, made of grass with a door of woven reeds. On either side stands an upright bundle of tall, polished reeds. Far back is a tiny grass shrine. NDAGIRE *and* NATTU *are sitting on a wild animal's hide in front of the tent. They gaze in silence at something in the distance. It is sunset.*

NATTU: There, sister, the setting sun ends another day of our exile.

NDAGIRE: Very true, my sister; and we are not very different from that setting sun: just as he has lost his light and heat, folded his dazzling legs within himself and become a mere ball, so have we, royal princesses once, been forced to slave like maids, away in this bush.

NATTU: I'm so tired of this bush. This bush, left and right, surrounding us—not a single proper house in sight, not even one banana tree to console one's eyes. Whoever thought when we were amid the splendours of the palace that we should ever lead such miserable lives?

NDAGIRE: This slavery is what I hate most. How can we, a king's daughters, be made to serve a commoner, an ordinary woman?

NATTU: I had thought, sister, that our service would be honourable, though hard. Our luck, though it has changed now, was unique when we were chosen from among so many princesses to serve the King on this campaign.

NDAGIRE: Oh, my little, simple sister! Don't you see that since the King has turned slave to his wife, by serving him we are only slaving for Nannono's slave? It's just the opposite of what I had hoped for. I thought we came as royal ladies to wait upon the King, our brother, while his maid served us; but now we slave for the maid! I will do it no more. If Nannono can make our brother drunk with her flirtatious tricks and lies, she cannot ever enslave me.

NATTU: I don't understand. What do you mean?

NDAGIRE: Don't you see? Nannono enjoys this life; she glories in it. She has no rival here for the King's bed; she has a husband all to herself. She orders the King about as if *he* were wife to her; and so she keeps him here, prevents his fighting, for that would mean the end of the war, and of her monopoly over him. And he, our poor brother, thinks she's right and obeys when she tells him to wait. He's caught in her trap, our brother; his heart is chained in her cunning bonds. Her selfishness, he thinks, is love.

NATTU: Poor Nakibinge and all his men! They came to fight this enemy here invading our land, and now they hang up their spears and shields just because a woman has aims beyond their knowledge.

MPISI *enters and approaches them cautiously.*

NDAGIRE: I pity myself first. If he is not—

MPISI (*bending close to* NDAGIRE's *ear*): May I—

NDAGIRE: Huuu! Who are you? What are you? You scared me!

MPISI: I apologize, my honoured lady.

NDAGIRE: Apologies do not mend matters. What are you looking for while all your fellow warriors are drilling before the
   King?

MPISI: May I, my honoured lady—?

NDAGIRE: Down on your knees, you impertinent boy! (MPISI
   kneels.) You call me 'honoured lady' while you address me
   standing!

MPISI: I . . . I beg your pardon, my lady, I didn't mean to offend
   you. May I rob you of this honoured lady's company for a
   while? I have an urgent message for her from my master,
   your uncle.

NDAGIRE: I will not for any reason have men buzzing like flies
   round my sister.

MPISI: But, my lady, it's from her uncle.

NDAGIRE: Who's supposed to be looking after her—her uncle
   or I?

MPISI: He sent me. He told me to bring the message.

NDAGIRE: Say what you came to tell her, then, and be gone. I
   don't see that any message can have been important enough
   for you to miss the parade.

NATTU: What is the message, Mpisi?

MPISI: My honoured lady, the message is sealed with secrecy.

NDAGIRE: What? And you expect me to approve of such things?

NATTU: Let's not delay him, sister; the King may be coming
   back any time now.

NDAGIRE: Are you then interested in what he has to say?

NATTU (*hesitating*): Yes, I'm not sure what it is.

NDAGIRE (*sighing*): There, then, waste no more time, young man.

NATTU: Step aside and tell me. My uncle has hardly ever sent
   to me before. (*They move away*.) What does he say?

MPISI: Did you believe my little lie? Your uncle has sent no

D

word; I had to invent a tale for your royal sister because I was embarrassed to find her here. I thought she would have accompanied the King to the parade and would have left you alone at home. (NDAGIRE *moves behind the hut*.)

NATTU: If this wilderness can be called home! But the King seems to prefer his maid's company now, and my sister is unhappy: she is tired of this bush life and your delay in ending the war.

MPISI: But that's the King's fault—if I may say so, my lady. He delays action. Let him allow us but one battle and we will rout the enemy. I can never understand why he checked us that day when we had driven the enemy right out of their camp: we could have ended the war there and then, and victoriously too.

NATTU: Ndagire, my sister, says it's all the Lady Nannono's doing; that she holds the King back from battle.

MPISI: But how can a mere woman hinder a King?

NATTU: Life is full of contradictions. You may not attach much importance to a mere woman—

MPISI: I-I-I didn't say that, my lady.

NATTU: Perhaps not: but you may think a woman like the Lady Nannono doesn't mean very much to the King; but when she's the only woman he has instead of his normal twenty wives, she really counts for a great deal, and can easily lord it over him.

MPISI: It's strange.

NATTU: Yes, and sad, and annoying too: to see that a king who left his palace and came to drive an enemy out of his land is turned slave to a cunning woman—at least, so my sister tells me. We are all ruled by the Lady Nannono: the army, we royal princesses, and the King himself. We are disgusted with this woman's usurped rule, and this wild life.

MPISI: Of course, my lady, every single soul in this camp is sick of it.

NATTU: The Lady Nannono is not.

MPISI: Maybe not her, but everyone else is: no hope, no wives, no beer, nothing. And that's what I came to talk to you about, my honoured lady. You remember the night when we danced here in the full moon? I suggested to you the idea of flight and you said you would think about it.

NATTU: And I have been thinking.

MPISI: May I learn the outcome of your thinking, my lady? You know the dark will reach its peak tonight; the new moon may appear in a day or two. But we can use tonight to fly and get out of this hateful wilderness. The dark of night, they say, is the poor man's travelling time.

NATTU: It isn't as easy as all that, Mpisi. Remember I am a royal princess; I'm difficult to hide. We may fly under the dark of night, but where would you put me when day came? And don't think I'll disappear and have no one tracing my steps.

MPISI: Oh, let's be practical, my lady; we can easily—

GUNJU *rushes in.* NATTU *screams and clings to* MPISI.

GUNJU: What is this, Mpisi? How dare you touch a woman on drilling day? (NATTU *lets go of* MPISI.) And you, a man from my company!

MPISI: My lord, I am not taking part in the drill.

GUNJU: Indeed! You are then guilty of two crimes: the sacrilege of defiling yourself on a sacred day; and then absenting yourself from the parade. And the stuff you talk to this girl!

NATTU: I am a princess, sir.

GUNJU: I'm sorry: the nonsense you talk to this honoured lady!

MPISI: So you've been eavesdropping.

GUNJU: How dare you say such a thing? I just heard . . . Eavesdropping indeed! Dare you be so insolent when you know this sort of behaviour can cost you your life? Can you guess what would happen if I told the King that you have not attended the parade?

NATTU: But you are not attending the parade yourself, sir.

GUNJU: Eh?

MPISI: Yes, yes, yes; you want to frighten me when you—

GUNJU: Behave yourself, dog. I possess the power to have you killed, and no one—

NDAGIRE returns quickly from behind the hut.

NDAGIRE: Nattu, the King's coming back. I hear the horn.

GUNJU runs off, followed by MPISI.

Oh, oh, the cowards! How they fly like deer before the hunter's horn.

NATTU: Is the King coming? I cannot hear anything.

NDAGIRE: The King is nowhere near. The horn hooted in my imagination. I just wished to wrench you away from those growling dogs.

NATTU: I hate that old man, the chief.

NDAGIRE: Of course, it is the nature of youth to hate age, as if it weren't the destination to which youth itself hurries. But you know, my sister, you must learn to check yourself. Youth is a blessed time: you're lovely and loved, and able to love, yourself. But youth is also a curse: the limbs are quick, but the brains are dull in youth. If you expose yourself like this to everyone who appears, you can only expect to reap tears from your youth.

NATTU: But when men come to me, especially young men, I can't help pitying them: they seem so lonely.

NDAGIRE: Of course, of course, our men deserve our pity—and why should I be bothering you about such things, telling you to keep away from men, when all our tribe is suffering just because the King is trapped by a woman? My sister, I wish you shared my grief for this: to suffer, sigh and long for home because a woman, a wretched woman, wants to feed her lust upon the King. No, I can't endure this folly any more. Tonight I will warn the King. I will not serve his bitch a day longer: I am a princess.

Enter a MAN blowing a horn, and then another carrying NANNONO on his shoulders.

NATTU: The King returns. But no, it's Nannono. See how she rides on men's shoulders like a princess.

NDAGIRE: And we who are princesses are made to walk; and she is heralded by horns as if she weren't a commoner's daughter.

NANNONO (*stepping down*): Good. Tell the King to come home at once. He shouldn't stay out after sunset.

MAN: Yes, your ladyship.

Exit MAN.

NANNONO (*strutting up to them*): Your ladyships, you seem to be in very low spirits tonight.

NDAGIRE: So would you be if you'd once been in our place and had then been subjected to this treatment, just because one person has petty, base, selfish, frivolous aims.

NANNONO: Frivolous? Do you mean the King's aim of expelling the invader from his land is frivolous?

NDAGIRE: Do not put words in my mouth; and in any case, whatever the King's aims are, if the King can have any aims by this time, they do not concern me. All I want is the immediate end of the war and my immediate return to where I belong. I'm tired of this role of maid-servant: I was never born to serve.

NANNONO: I understand, my honoured ladies. You know, I truly feel for you both, royal princesses: I feel I should be serving you, and I'm ashamed to be served by you, superior to me by nothing less than a King's own blood. But, you know, my ladies, I can't do anything about it. The King orders and we have to obey; he prevents me from serving you; and he orders you to serve me.

NDAGIRE: That's why I'm disgusted with this life, where I have to obey revolutionary ideas. I will not see my grandfather's traditions turned upside down.

NANNONO: Traditions? But a king is not bound by traditions. His orders are the law.

NDAGIRE (*rises*): I have to collect herbs for your basin. My role of queen-sister has been turned into that of housemaid. (*Goes behind the hut.*)

NANNONO: Your sister's cross tonight.

NATTU: She says you have played a great part in delaying the ending of the war . . . but, please, don't tell her I said this.

NANNONO: Oh come, my girl: I know a little better than that. What use would it be telling her? Tell a leopard he's cruel, a hyena he's greedy, or a goat he's stupid! Your sister knows her own mind best.

NATTU: That then is what she says: delight in having the King all to yourself makes you urge him to keep away from battle and to prolong the war.

NANNONO: So! Her guess is close to the truth, but certainly not charitable. It's base and odious nonsense to think that I, Nannono, hold the King from action because I want to enjoy a monopoly over his body. Nattu, I'll tell you the heart of the matter. You are young and your way of thinking is nearer to my own. Your sister is already a hag and she may well behave as if she had never been in love.

NATTU: Love, did you say?

NANNONO: Yes, sister. The King and I have come across a sweet and blessed secret.

NATTU: What's that?

NANNONO: A secret, I said. You know, at the palace, when the King was surrounded by his queens and maids, and came to me only once every month, we could not really learn what joy there can be between husband and wife; but now we've found it: we've found that man and woman can live in more exalted bliss than ever we thought. We've found in each other charms which when at home we couldn't discover. And the King would not change this life for all the world: these woods, he says, are sweeter to him than all the splendours of the palace, the tall grass and the giant trees here are more delightful to him than all the banana groves of the villages; the bark of the fox and the hyena's laugh are more enchanting than the music of all his court bands, he says . . . and I, as a loyal subject and humble maid to him, would not rob him of his joy. But what your sister thinks is arrant nonsense: that I, Nannono, should keep the King from battle because I want to enjoy his body!

NATTU: I understand; and I feel you're right; for what use is it to rule the world, or to have all the pleasures of life if love is not among your possessions?

NANNONO: Yes, that's what the King said to me last night. He said he has come to the fountain of . . . (*She turns excitedly as a horn sounds.*) O, hear the horn! The King is coming home.

Enter TWO MEN *blowing horns, followed by another carrying the* KING *on his shoulders.*

NANNONO: My lord. . . . (*She walks towards the* KING, *who steps down.*)

KING: Can't you see my maid has difficulty with her dress, Nattu? (NATTU *follows* NANNONO *and holds up the train of her dress.*)

NANNONO (*kneeling on hide*): I was almost getting cross with you, my lord, for staying away so long.

KING (*sitting and leaning his head against* NANNONO): Oh, I enjoyed the parade: so many men performing so beautifully. I felt almost certain at that moment that I could defeat the whole world with such an army.

NANNONO: Of course, my lord, your army can defeat any enemy, provided you are with them. What battle have you fought and lost? Jjuma, your rebel brother, flew before you like dry leaves before the hot season's wind; and that Kimyanku, they tell me, fled like a rabbit from the hunter's dogs when you advanced towards him like a river flood upon the marsh grass, although you had lost Wanema's son, the war-god.

KING: Ah, yes, that victory which brought you to me as a gift from your father: when I thought I would never get a greater woman than Bukirwa Nanzigu, who sacrificed her only son

to appease Wanema, when his son had been killed in my
wars.

Groans and wailing off-stage.

NANNONO: What's that?

KING: I wonder! . . . Ah, I understand now. It's the men to be
sacrificed to Kibuuka. How they groan like women!

NATTU: Fear and death make no distinction between man and
woman, or between brave men and cowards. These two
reduce us all to equality.

KING: Ha, Nattu, what do you mean? You think I am going to
be equal with the peasants when I die? Never . . . even my
tomb will be called a shrine, while theirs will be mere plain,
unknown graves.

Enter two EXECUTIONERS *dragging along two* PRISONERS.

EXECUTIONERS (*kneeling before* KING *and making gestures of grati-
tude*): Tweyanze, tweyanze! These, our lord, are Kibuuka's
victims.

1ST PRISONER: Oh King! Oh master of life and death? Spare us,
oh King!

2ND PRISONER: Oh ruler of all . . .

EXECUTIONER (*kicking him*): How dare you touch the King
with your foul hands?

KING *goes to shrine, takes out a plate-like basket and raises it; puts
it back and returns. He takes one of the executioner's spears and
taps each prisoner lightly on the back of the neck. Fresh and louder
groans.*

EXECUTIONERS (*gesturing with their spears towards the* KING): We
are your faithful servants. We appease the gods. Remember
us on the day of the victory. (*Exeunt with* PRISONERS.)

KING: I wish I were really master of life and death, as these
victims of flames call me. It is a real burden to me to have to

murder my fellow human beings, just because there are gods to please.

NANNONO: But those were prisoners from the enemy.

KING: Yes, but as human beings, they are more related to me than any gods.

NANNONO: In any case, you brought the gods onto the scene. You could have fought quite successfully without that Kibuuka.

KING: I tell you, my maid, it's impossible. I've fought long enough now to know that man, without the help of the gods, cannot sway the fortunes of war. (NDAGIRE *returns from behind the hut.*) I've tried many times to forget all about the gods, but . . .

NDAGIRE: Your basin is ready for your bath.

NANNONO: Oh, thank you very much, my lady.

NDAGIRE: Do I deserve thanks? It's part of my duties, as queen-sister, to serve you. (NANNONO *walks towards hut. The* KING *tries to follow.*)

NDAGIRE: My lord!

KING: Yes. (NANNONO *goes behind the hut.*)

NDAGIRE: I would like to talk to you. Where were you go-ing now? Won't you leave your wife alone even at her bath?

KING: Ha, ha, ha! Is that what you want to talk to me about? I see no danger in my presence at Nannono's bath. Does she have any secrets to keep from me?

NDAGIRE: Please, let us turn to more serious matters.

KING: What is it, sister? You shouldn't be so upset by tiny things. . . . Now you've frightened my maid.

NDAGIRE: Nattu, please, will you go and light a fire inside. (NATTU *enters hut.*) I don't know, Nakibinge, what you mean by your tiny things. But if you mean that my feelings are trifles, let me tell you that all your tribe has become a little thing to you, because my feelings are the feelings of the whole of your tribe. Understand me, Nakibinge: I speak to you as sister to brother, and so listen like my dead mother's son. Why, my brother, why in the name of all the gods of this land, why should you keep us and your men for months and months in these wild wastes by delaying a battle which you know must be fought sooner or later? Why should all the men in our tribe live like widowers, why all the women lament like widows, why should all the children be orphans, just because you won't fight one battle, drive the enemy out of here and end the war?

KING: I'm quite aware of the grief which my delay is causing to my people, my sister. But I feel my delay is necessary, because, although I trust the courage of my men, I have no reason to trust their skill. More than half of my army in this camp are fresh recruits, young men who have never fought in battle before, and I am sure this is going to be the strongest challenge we are to face. I want my men to have some practice before I—

NDAGIRE: Now, Nakibinge, be frank with me, and with yourself. Do not try to veil the truth from me, because I already know everything.

KING: I beg your pardon!

NDAGIRE: I said I know everything. I am absolutely sure Nannono is keeping you away from battle. She prevents you from fighting. No, no, no—let me speak. I know you love your maid, and you want to do her will. But that would be a betrayal of both your men and your manhood. You are the King, my brother, and you must lead your people; you can't be ordered about by a woman. . . . It's all very strange, brother. I can't really understand, but I feel it. Your mind is growing weak. At your palace, you have more than twenty wives all to yourself, and they love and obey you. But all of them could not with their tears and charms prevent you from coming to war—because then you knew your royal duties. But this one scheming girl to capture your mind like this, and make you a slave to her wicked wishes!

KING: No, that's nonsense, Ndagire. You insult me to say I am ruled by a woman, and you falsely accuse my maid.

NDAGIRE: Well, I have told you my feelings, and as I said, they are the feelings of all your tribe. Things are getting desperate: I wouldn't be surprised if your men even revolted against you. And this girl you are doting on will very shortly, with that thing growing inside her, be utterly useless to you. (*Goes into the hut.*)

KING: Yes, that is what it is: the deceit of this world. The body deceives you: you think the more you supply its desires the more it will become subject to you, and yet it grows more wild, more rebellious. With twenty wives, I thought I had too few; then I got disillusioned: I've found much more joy with only one, Nannono, my little maid. The months I have spent with her alone in this wilderness have been the happiest of all my life. But now bitterness comes again: I have to fight—and plunge again into that herd of my wives, and forget my joy, sacrifice it to petty bodily pleasures. And this woman, Ndagire, like all other fools, misinterprets my thoughts. . . . My gods!

NANNONO (*returning, rubbing her arms and shoulders*): Ah, the water was so cold. What did your sister tell you? She has been so queer to me tonight. What, are you sulking too? Are you snubbing me? O salty flood of tears, fill my heart and overflow through my eyes.

KING (*holding* NANNONO): Oh, no, my little maid! I am not snubbing you. I was only trying to think.

NANNONO (*softly*): What were you trying to think? Cold reason, you know, is hostile to sweet thoughts. Reason and love will never share the same bed in man's heart.

KING: Reason and what?

NANNONO: And love, I said. (*She puts an arm round* KING's *neck.*) You know, I told Nattu today—

KING (*drawing away*): Told who? Have you, then, disclosed our secret?

NANNONO: No, my lord, but. . . . Let's sit down. I'm feeling very cold.

KING: Let's go in, then. It's even getting dark.

NANNONO: No, please. Spare me your sister's company for a while. Let's walk here. This evening breeze is the best nourishment of sweet thoughts. (*They walk arm in arm.*)

KING: But I have no more sweet feelings, my little maid.

NANNONO: What, my lord, what's wrong? Are you still worried about Kibuuka's human victims?

KING: No, my little maid. It's the very thing you call sweet thoughts that worries me now.

NANNONO: Our love? Are you getting tired of it? Such a new gift?

KING: No, but my sense of duty tells me I must lay it aside for a time and fight this necessary battle.

NANNONO: I don't understand, my lord.

KING: I said I feel it's high time I fought the enemy.

NANNONO: Say, my lord, it is time you hate me. Is this what it is to trust kings?

KING (*painfully*): My little maid!

NANNONO: No, there's nothing more to it; how could you fail to see this? That your fighting means the grave of our love, that it must end the days of our bliss—how could you fail to see that?

KING: I see everything, my little maid, and that's why I said I am deeply grieved. As I told you, Nannono, I would not change this life for all the world; I would not change you for all the wealth of my land. I would not change you for all the matrons and maids of my tribe. Because what I feel for you is . . .

NANNONO: It's love. I know that is what I feel for you, my lord.

KING: Well, whatever it is, I cannot have the sweetness of this life any more, since it cannot be found amid the noise and bustle of my palace: I cannot find it there.

NANNONO: Of course, you can't. You would even forget that I

had ever existed once you returned to your herd of wives. Do you desire this?

KING: Oh no! My little maid. I will never desire anything but you.

NANNONO: Why, then, my lord, are you so eager to end the war and return to the place you hate?

KING: Duty calls me, my sweet maid. It's a cursed burden to be King, Nannono. These frail shoulders of mine can't. . .

NANNONO: Your shoulders are not frail, Nakibinge; don't belittle yourself.

KING: I know they wouldn't be frail for an ordinary man, who has no more cares than those of himself and his love. But mine are too frail for a King: too weak to support all the responsibilities of my realm. Every single life in this land, Nannono, with all its cares and worries, hangs round my neck, just because I was cursed with the name of King. And it is this ill luck that forces me to murder our love; and to take you back to that palace, where we shall forget each other, and I will turn servant to my wicked body again. Because once I fight, the war will end, and then there will be no further excuse for my staying away from the palace. But fight I must, and now. All my men are getting bored and desperate.

NANNONO: Come, my lord, that's a childish argument. If you say that your men are getting bored, don't forget that the enemy is getting bored too; and there's no reason why you cannot outwait him. Your men should be able to resist more than the enemy. They are in their own land, and with you, their King. The invaders, I understand, have got only a few representatives from their King.

KING: That's true.

NANNONO: Why then are you so eager to fight and end the only real days of your life?

KING: Nannono, I've told you duty compels me; and there are other reasons besides. (*Points at* NANNONO's *belly.*) Now our baby will be coming soon; your days are drawing near. And I would not like you to have that baby, the child who will be my heir, in these wild, rough surroundings.

NANNONO: Oh come, my lord! Where there's love, there's enough. Do not worry about me. Why, all the creatures in this wilderness have their babies here, and they bring them up here. Do not bother yourself, my lord: if you speak of duty, remember that love, as we have experienced it, is the first duty, and all other things can wait. Do not hasten to defeat the enemy and then return to that enclosure of flattery where love can never blossom. (*Strolling dreamily, hand in hand.*) Here let's live, and here let's love, as long as time allows. . . .

After some moments KAGALI *and* JITA *rush in.*

KAGALI: My lord King, my lord!

KING: I'm here, Kagali, what's the matter?

KAGALI: We're being attacked, my lord. The enemy are surrounding the camp.

KING: How far are they? Already at the camp?

KAGALI: No, but the watchmen saw them about a thousand paces away.

KING: Well, then, we arm and go. You blow the horns and collect all the men at the musizi tree in front of the camp. I will arm and be with you in a moment.

JITA: But, my lord, shall we. . . .

KING: Come, no more delay. You go and collect the men.

KAGALI *and* JITA *go off. A fanfare of horns, gradually fading as* NANNONO *walks up to the* KING.

KING (*taking her hand*): It has come, my sweet maid. It has come: at last I have to fight.

NANNONO (*upset*): The gods and spirits decide so. Fight well. But we can stay here after the war. I wish. . . . No, I have no wishes.

KING (*putting an arm round her*): Oh, do wish! Wish that I defeat the enemy.

NANNONO: That I know you will; and by defeating them you will defeat our love as well.

KING: I am not so sure this time. I've never been more nervous about battle before. I am frightened. (*Several* MEN *enter.*)

MAN: What's this coming at night?

KING: It's battle.

MEN: The King, the King! (*They kneel.*)

KING: Join your comrades before the camp. I'm coming in a moment.

MEN (*rising and gesturing with spears towards the* KING): For you, our lord, we will fight. Death rather than defeat.

Exeunt.

NANNONO: Do not be frightened, Nakibinge. You've never lost a battle, and you are not going to begin now.

KING: You never know, my dear. The best boatman usually drowns in the lake, and the best warrior falls in battle. . . . But, in case the terrible thing happens—

NANNONO: Oh, may all the gods and spirits of our land prevent it!

KING: But, in case it happens, my little maid, (*draws her close*) in case it happens, remember my will: that baby you are expecting must be my heir: it must be King after me. And until it is born, *you* are going to rule my people.

NANNONO: That's a strange decision, my lord. I am only a woman, and the baby may be a girl.

KING: Well, if the baby is a girl, they will choose who will rule them. But as for you, you must rule my tribe until your baby is born—if I fall in this battle. I will tell the chiefs my mind. I am the King and I am the law.

NANNONO: Anyway, I trust the need will not arise. You will fight and return to my arms alive. Let's go in and arm you. (*They turn to go.*)

Blackout

Horns sound and men shout; the noise rises to a crescendo, then slowly fades. Light returns to the stage, strong and bright. It is late morning. NANNONO, NATTU *and* NDAGIRE *sit at the door of the tent.*

NANNONO: The morning is now gone and no news is come to ease our hearts. I can hardly remember another battle so long: fighting from night to noon without a break!

NDAGIRE: I would urge our men to fight for months without a break once I knew they were fighting for the liberation of our land, as they are doing now.

NATTU: Yes, and to secure our return home.

NDAGIRE: Nannono would rather stop them, I'm sure: even now when all is going well.

NANNONO: I? Never. I even wish I had the chance myself to fight. O, by all the spirits of war, if only I could I would stand by my King and fight till I won or fell. I would . . . (MPISI *rushes in, startling the ladies.*) What's this? Where are you running to, little man?

MPISI: We're lost, my gentle ladies, we're lost. We've fought through the night and the morning: but the enemy pours in still, hordes and hordes of them, numbers we never expected.

NANNONO: Is the King alive?

MPISI: Yes, and still fighting, but the situation is hopeless.

NANNONO: Is that why you're running away and abandoning your King?

MPISI: We've no more spears. Remaining on the field now is giving oneself away to certain death. There's no hope.

NANNONO: O coward! You wretched mouse of a man! How dare you run away from your King's and your tribe's service? What is your life compared to that of the King? Is this what we expect from you? Is this the news your wife awaits to receive? Is this going to be her reward for her long loneliness and the cold chills of an unshared bed? Shame on you!

MPISI: My lady, I return to battle to die.

NANNONO (*pulls him back*): Wait: you are utterly useless there. Did you say you had no more spears?

MPISI: None, my lady. Even the King does not have one.

NANNONO: Quick, then, pull down those reeds. (MPISI *pulls down pillar on right*.) Get a knife, quick. (NATTU *gives* NANNONO *a knife. She sharpens a number of reeds*.) Here, take these and give them to the King and tell him to use them as spears . . . and come back immediately for more . . . and conduct yourself like one of the heroes of your tribe. Go. (*Exit* MPISI, *with reeds*.) Come, my ladies, get knives and help. (NDAGIRE *comes and helps* NANNONO *to sharpen reeds. As* NATTU *comes down too, enter two* MEN).

1ST MAN: More reeds, my ladies: they work wonderfully. The King demands more.

2ND MAN: And sends thanks to you for your resourcefulness, my lady.

NANNONO: Thanks will come later; duty now: take these. (MEN *take reeds and go*.) This is going to be the most brilliant victory in our history: a battle fought with reeds.

NDAGIRE: I hope we win at last.

NANNONO (*walking to pillar on the left*): Come, let's pull these down as well. (*Shouts* . . . KAGALI, JITA *and some five men run in*.) What's this, my lords? Are you abandoning your King?

JITA: Oh, no, my lady! There's no King any more to abandon.

3 LADIES: What? No King?

JITA: No King. Our Lord has withdrawn his hand from his shield. He's dead. LADIES *sink, wailing* . . . MEN *bring in some wounded warriors, among whom is* GUNJU, *who groans loudly*.)

KAGALI: My ladies, we cannot wait. The enemy have routed our army, and we have to get away from here. The remnant of our forces is already across the river, and we must catch up with them now, before the enemy is upon us.

NANNONO: How did the King die?

JITA: An arrow pierced his breast, my lady.

NATTU: And what were you all doing not to shield him?

NANNONO: Where's the King's body? (*Rises.*) Where is it?

JITA: Madam, we couldn't reach it. We were fighting near a deep ditch, and when he was struck; he fell into the ditch.

NANNONO: O foul death! O shameful death! O most wretched end for a King! A King's annointed body to rot graveless among the foul corpses of hostile warriors!

GUNJU: Oh, I die. Kagali, Kagali, my friend. I die, come. . . . I die, my friend. Console my wives and my children, and all my relatives. Tell them I fell by my K—

KAGALI: He's gone. . . . There in death can we see our life as it really is, a sound without an echo, a wave that melts on the lake's edge.

NDAGIRE (*raising* NATTU): Come, my father's daughter. The days of our rule are past. We go home to fall into obscure shadows. We know now how much a woman can sway the fortunes of a nation. Narrators will invent explanations for this, but never find the right one—woman.

NANNONO: You are gone, my love: Where shall I remain? A kingless queen, a pregnant widow. Whose child will this you leave in me be called? And yet I feel I caused your death. I held your hand from bloody battle to have our love mature. But the enemy made the fatal plans. . . . By loving I have lost the only thing I loved. (*Shouts off stage.*)

KAGALI (*rushing to* NANNONO): They're here my lady. Let's fly. (*Sweeps her off and exit, carrying her: all the rest follow.*)

Blackout.

Light on GUNJU's *body and*

Curtain

The Trick

a one-act play based on
'The Shadow of the Glen' by J. M. Synge
transposed into an African setting

ERISA KIRONDE

Characters

KALEKEZI
MUSICIAN
KAMULI   Wife of Kalekezi
KAZUNGU   A herdsman

The inside of a rectangular hut. A fire-place is in one corner, lying on the fire-stones there is a covered pot. A kettle nestles between two of the stones. There is also a bundle of firewood in the fire-place corner.

Near the fire-place is a pot containing waragi, banana wine, which stands on a pad of banana leaves and is covered by another similar pad. Three or four short logs, serving as stools, are placed around the interior. There is also a reed table on which are scattered two china cups, two jam tins and some enamel plates. An enamel basin leans against one of the walls. The hut has one entrance up stage; the door is of reed. At one end of the hut is a bed of reeds on which lies the body of KALEKEZI, *covered with a blanket.*

As the play opens KAMULI *is seen, lit only by firelight, counting currency notes. She places them carefully into a wallet.*

The MUSICIAN *calls softly from outside the hut.* KAMULI *hurriedly stuffs the money and the wallet into her bodice. She lights a lamp from the fire and opens the door.*

MUSICIAN: Good evening, owner of the house.

KAMULI: Good evening, friend. It is dark and you are hills away from the next village.

MUSICIAN: It is, but I walk from Nalubabwe and back to Nalubabwe.

KAMULI: On your feet?

MUSICIAN: On my feet, owner of the house, and when I see a house, I call, and say to myself, 'Maybe they'll give me a piece of cassava and a corner for my drum, and maybe they'd enjoy my jesting.' So . . . (*Looks in past her and sees dead man.*) . . . but . . . not yours. I see you are in sadness.

KAMULI: No matter, stranger. (*Sighs.*) No matter, bring your drum in.

MUSICIAN (*slowly in and towards bed*): Dead?

KAMULI: Dead. He has died on me. And I in a foreign land and with all the cotton ready to be picked and the coffee trees just ready to start yielding.

MUSICIAN: He looks queer for a dead man.

KAMULI: He was always queer when he was alive. I wouldn't expect him to change in death.

MUSICIAN: But why let him lie there dead and not stretch him? He will grow cold on your hands.

KAMULI: I am afraid, friend. For he put a black curse on me only this morning, that if he died suddenly and I touched or let anyone touch his body except his sister, Sirisita—and she is many hills away—I would never sleep again.

MUSICIAN: A queer story. Not let his own woman touch him. A queer story.

KAMULI: He was a queer man and an old man. A queer man, never in the house and always thinking of his childhood and of his people. (*Pulls back a bit of the blanket.*) . . . lay your hand on him and tell me if he is cold.

MUSICIAN: And not sleep again, owner of the house, and not sleep again? I wouldn't touch him for all Byandala's cattle.

KAMULI: Maybe he's cold but not dead. He was always cold—

all the time I've known him. But I think he is dead. This morning he was to walk to Nalubabwe, to sell his waragi. But then he didn't. He went into his bed and started moaning about his home and brothers and sisters and childhood he would not see again, and, as the sun went down behind the hills, he told me to watch and tell him when it disappeared. When I told him, he let out a cry, as if his grandfather's spirits were on him, and stiffened out like cold food.

MUSICIAN: Eeeee. Give me some water.

KAMULI (*taking bottle from behind firewood and pouring him half a cup of waragi**): Maybe that would quench your thirst better than the dew of the morning.

MUSICIAN: If he wasn't lying there and growing cold, I would play you thanks on my drum. Thank you. (*Drinks.*)

KAMULI: Sit down, stranger, sit and rest, and I will finish feeding this fire and will feed us.

MUSICIAN: I have walked the whole country but I never saw a woman stay the whole night alone with a dead body.

KAMULI: But didn't I tell you of the curse and that he only died at sunset and the neighbours so far away. Tomorrow I shall fetch his sister and tell the neighbours. I bring the curse on me if anyone but Sirisita touches him and how could I go out in the dark now so many hills and leave him alone?

MUSICIAN: No offence meant.

KAMULI: None taken. But how would you know what it's like to be a woman, a woman without child, and married to an old drunk, and hills and hills away from the neighbours— foreign neighbours at that?

MUSICIAN: And I had thought I would be turned away from here too. I live on the road and many times am turned away by those who think me a thief or a madman.

KAMULI (*too quickly*): I have nothing to lose. Most nights I am lonely. Tonight I was lonely and afraid.

---

* waragi—locally made gin. Government has now taken over the manufacturing of this intoxicating drink.

MUSICIAN: Of him?

KAMULI: Of him. But you, aren't you ever lonely or afraid?

MUSICIAN: Me. Afraid? Lonely? I am too poor and homeless to feel lonely, and walking the roads at night, turned away from doors, where would I be if I felt afraid? If I were easily frightened, walking in the night with every bush a lion, every falling leaf a leopard, and every stray branch a snake and all the town robbers on the road every night. If I were afraid, I'd be a madman . . . shouted at by all the village children or maybe dead . . . like Mukasa who was found on the hills.

KAMULI: You knew him?

MUSICIAN: Knew him? I was the last man heard his voice.

KAMULI: How was it? There were strange tales but who can believe the rumours we hear.

MUSICIAN: Strange it was and I'm not lying. It was a closed-eyes night just like this and I walking along as I was tonight and I heard a voice so weird calling out such strange things that I ran and I ran till I came to the next village and got drunk as quickly as I could. I got drunk the next morning and the next. I'd some money from a wedding I was playing at—and the third day they found him. And then I knew it was no ghost I was hearing and came alive again.

KAMULI: I knew Mukasa. He'd always turn in to greet me whenever he passed if I was hoeing . . . and I was very sad when he died . . . for a long time, till I got used to being lonely again. (*Stands up.*) Did you pass anyone on the road?

MUSICIAN: Only Kazungu driving the cattle he'd bought today.

KAMULI: Kazungu. Did you meet him? How far down the road?

MUSICIAN: Not far. He must be nearly passing here now.

KAMULI: Well, if you are not afraid, feed this fire till I come back.

MUSICIAN: I will. A man that's dead can't hurt me.

KAMULI: I am going to see Kazungu. He has a small shed near

here where he sleeps his cattle on market days. He will tell
Sirisita that my man is dead.

MUSICIAN: Let me go and tell him. It's dark and you don't like
the dark. (*Looking at body.*)

KAMULI: You wouldn't find the way. I'll go. If you want your
supper, mind that fire.

MUSICIAN: Maybe you have a needle and a bit of thread and I'll
mend my rags while you're gone.

KAMULI (*taking a needle from a bit of cloth and fishing out some thread*):
Here, stranger. This should take your mind off the dead man
while I am away.

Exit KAMULI.

MUSICIAN *begins stitching and breaks into song, but, remembering
where he is, stops. The blanket is drawn slowly off the body.*
KALEKEZI *looks out.* MUSICIAN *moves uneasily, then looks up and
springs to his feet with a movement of terror.*

KALEKEZI: Don't be afraid, Majangwa. A man that's dead can't
hurt you.

MUSICIAN: It was you all the time, was it? Waragi and Nalubabwe should have told me. But you are dead. Have I made you
angry?

A long whistle from outside and from KALEKEZI.

KALEKEZI: That woman! Is it any tribe's custom for a woman
to whistle? I'm not dead but dying of thirst. Bring me a drop
quickly before she comes back.

MUSICIAN: Then you're not dead?

KALEKEZI: How could I die, and I as dry as a rubbing stone?

MUSICIAN (*going behind firewood and bringing out bottle, pouring out
liberal measure of waragi in a cup*): What will she say if she
notices you smell like a beer-boat? You must have a reason
for pretending to be dead?

KALEKEZI: I have, Majangwa, and I shall show myself soon, for my joints are going to sleep and there's been a fly on my nose as big as a bat and making me want to sneeze . . . and you two nattering away like weaver birds about leopards and Mukasa (curse him) and coffee. Give me that waragi. Will you wait till she comes back before I've had a sip? (MUSICIAN *gives him cup and he drinks.*)

KALEKEZI: Go over now to where those spears are and fish out that stick.

MUSICIAN (*going*): This one, Kalekezi?

KALEKEZI: That's the one—an old friend—for I have a bad woman in my house.

MUSICIAN: But she's a fine woman, Kalekezi, and worried about the crops.

KALEKEZI: Worried about money, not the crops. Worried about money. (*Drinks.*) She's a bad wife. Just you stay here a little and I'll show you a thing or two . . . even if I am an old man, a queer man and a drunk.

MUSICIAN: There's a voice outside. (*Listens.*) No. Two voices, arguing.

KALEKEZI: Put that stick here on the bed and cover me over with the blanket and don't say anything of what you know or I shall die and see you get no more sleep. I wouldn't have told you if I hadn't been dying of thirst.

MUSICIAN: Shan't say a word, not one word. (*Goes back to fire and his mending.*)

KALEKEZI: Majangwa.

MUSICIAN: Sh . . . they're coming. They'll hear you.

Enter KAMULI *followed by* KAZUNGU, *a tall young man, dressed as a herdsman.*

KAMULI: I didn't take long, did I, friend?

MUSICIAN: You could have been quicker, owner of the house, you were long away.

KAMULI: There was no sign from him?

MUSICIAN: No sign at all.

KAMULI (*to* KAZUNGU): Go over, pull down the blanket and see for yourself.

KAZUNGU: I will not, Kamuli. I fear the dead. (*Sits on stool near the* MUSICIAN. KAMULI *takes kettle from fireplace, brings out paper packet of tea, measures it in her hand and pours into kettle, takes tin and cups off table.*)

KAMULI: Will you drink some tea with us, friend, or will you sleep? You must be tired with all your walking.

MUSICIAN: Sleep? With a dead man in the house? No, thank you. (*Drinks.*)

KAMULI (*examining cups*): But who has been drinking from this cup?

MUSICIAN: Is it dirty?

KAMULI: Smells of waragi. Have you helped yourself?

MUSICIAN: Would I use another cup if I had?

KAMULI: But it has been used. I left you here, with a dead man and a clean cup. The cup is dirty. Did the dead man use it?

MUSICIAN: You know your man better than I do. His spirit possibly.

KAZUNGU: Stranger things have happened. How unhandy you are with that needle and is it worth trying to mend such rags?

MUSICIAN: Maybe not, but I could answer about as worth while as you acting as herd to those cattle a while back, walking on the other side of the road without even a lamp.

KAMULI: Don't mind him. He has had too much and is already falling asleep.

KAZUNGU: I don't. And it's true the cattle gave me a hard trip. The calves running up the bank and into the maize on one side of the road and the bull running back at a lick the way he came. I thought I'd never get here and I dropped my lamp six miles back and couldn't find it in the dark.

KAMULI: The cattle of this part are hard to manage if you've not been born to it, like Mukasa, who knew every tick on their backs, the curve of each hump, and the droop of their horns.

MUSICIAN (*crossing from fire*): That was a fine man, young fellow.

He could tell all his calves if they were grazing with every cow in the village, and he could run from here to Mbarara and not get out of breath.

KAMULI: It's true and I like to hear you praise a dead man, whom none talks of now except to gossip about the way he died.

MUSICIAN: I've said nothing but what I know is true. (*Settles down as if to sleep.*)

KAZUNGU: The gossip today in the market said that you always spoke to Mukasa as he passed by.

KAMULI: That's true too.

KAZUNGU: You know an awful lot of men for a woman in a lonely place.

KAMULI: That's when you want to know them. You seize the chance to do more than greet anyone who's passing, and if I do know an awful lot of men, they're fine ones, for I've always been a hard woman to please . . . and I still am, let me warn you.

KAZUNGU: Were you hard to please when you took him?

KAMULI: He'd good land and money and who would look after me when I grow old if I didn't marry someone like that?

KAZUNGU: That's true and you looked ahead all right. He's a tidy bit of land and some good cotton and coffee. Cows would do well here and he must have left a bit of money.

KAMULI: I'm not sure I was wise. What good is rich land and cows and cotton when there's nothing to do but hoe in the garden, feed the fire and him, an old drunk man and a wife-beater. I just sit watching life go by.

KAZUNGU: What sort of talk is that?

KAMULI: The sort of talk you get to in a lonely place like this when most of the time you've nothing but yourself for company, waiting for the time when he'll come back rolling drunk again, and thinking of the women who were the best housewives when I was young and dancing. They're now old and useless and the children are growing up and will get a fine brideprice, who used to watch me with envy . . . and I sit here, getting older and nothing to show for it. (*Pulls wallet from bodice and begins counting it*.) What use is this money . . . 200 . . . without a man in the house . . . 300 . . . an empty house . . . 400 . . . and no children . . . 500 . . . and he dying on me . . . 800 . . . and the cotton unpicked . . . 900 and the coffee beginning to yield and . . . 40.

KAZUNGU: That's 950 . . . and you won't feel like that when you marry a young man and I'm not a fool at making a bargain, even if I got only four head in the market today. I'll make a profit even if the sellers want too much and the buyers pay too little. We'd do right to wait now till the old man is resting in his grave and all the rites are over, and some of the money gone to his family, and you've walked over the village with your hair wild and long . . . and then I'll move in and pick your coffee and take it to market . . . but we'd do right to wait.

KAMULI (*giving him waragi*): Why should I want to marry you any more than him? It won't be long before you'll be getting old and living for beer parties like him, and lying in your bed every night, smelling of drink, and snoring through your nose, with your teeth going bad and your hair dropping out. We'll all get old before we're done but it's not a pleasant thing to look forward to toothless gums, a wrinkled face and a doubled-up back and nothing to show for it.

KALEKEZI *begins slowly to sit up behind them.*

KAZUNGU: You've been living too long with an old man and you won't feel like that when you've a young man in the house.

KALEKEZI *sneezes.* KAZUNGU *tries to run to the door, but* KALEKEZI *jumps up, stick in hand, and goes over and puts his back to it.*

KALEKEZI: Now you won't wait till I'm rotting in my grave, till all the rites are over, and some of the money gone to my family, you won't wait till she's walked the villages with her hair wild and long . . . I'm going to give you something you won't have to wait for. (*Shaking stick.*)

KAZUNGU: Get me out of this, Kamuli. He always did what you told him. Get me out of this.

KAMULI (*looking at* MUSICIAN): Is he dead or living? Is he living?

KALEKEZI: You don't care whether I'm living or dead. But this is an end of your fine time and an end of your talking to the fine men who pass when you're digging. (*Opens door.*) Out you walk, Kamuli, and go on walking, and before long you too will be old and there'll be no more young men. They'll laugh at your toothless gums, Kamuli, and at your wrinkled face and your doubled-up back. They'll laugh and call you old woman.

KAMULI *looks at* KAZUNGU *who stirs uneasily.*

KAZUNGU: Maybe she could go back to her family.

KALEKEZI: They wouldn't take her back. No. She can just walk the hills till she dies and they pick up a shrivelled bundle of rags, and find another useless old woman is dead.

KAMULI: You won't be alive that day, Kalekezi. You'll have been a long time dead and good riddance. (*Changes tone and moves to him.*) Get back to bed. You're not well. Look, I've just made some tea and the food is about ready. Get back to your bed and I'll bring you some as I always do when you're drunk.

KALEKEZI (*snatching the money she still has in her hand*): Get out of that door and don't come back here. There's no food and no bed here for you.

MUSICIAN (*pointing to* KAZUNGU): Maybe he'd take her.

KAMULI: He'd have no use for me now.

MUSICIAN: But you'd have some use for him. He could give you half of a dry bed and good food in your mouth.

KALEKEZI: Do you call the man a fool or are you the fool? He

doesn't want her without my money. Out you go, Kamuli,
and you get out too, Majangwa. I'm tired of your chatter.

MUSICIAN: We'll be leaving you now. Come on, Kamuli. The
rain is falling but the air is kind and it'll be fine tomorrow.

KAMULI: What will it matter to me if it's fine or wet tomorrow,
and me with no roof over my head, and no food for my
stomach?

MUSICIAN: You'll not feel the lack of a roof when you're with
me for I know all the ways a man can to get food for his
stomach. We'll be going now and you'll learn how to live.
You were lonely married to an old man—and afraid. Come, I
will teach you to dismiss loneliness. We'll move from market
to market, and I'll play on my drum and you will dance and
the lonely, the bigger fools with homes, will pay for our act.

KALEKEZI (*impatiently*): Go out of that door, I tell you, and
make your plans outside.

KAMULI *gathers a few things.*

MUSICIAN (*at the door*): Come along with me and it's not only my
plans you'll hear but the laughter of the world will be ringing
in your ears. There'll be hard times of course. We'll get
turned away many a time from markets, and, when times are
hard and the cotton price has fallen, they'll let us sing and
dance and send us away with a dry lump of lumonde, but the
next market will put all straight. We'll be with people who
want to be happy and we'll delude them for a little time
longer into forgetfulness of their troubles, and, if the rain
wets us through, we'll see the sun rising over the hills and
the white mists flat over the swamps and the stars shining
till the shadow of every tree is plain. We'll watch the fools
who are afraid of life and we'll be living and you won't have
time to sit watching an old man snoring in his drunken sleep
and wheezing in his age.

KAMULI: I'll be wheezing myself by then in the cold swamp air,
I think. But you've a fine tongue, Majangwa, and a kindly

face. I'll come with you, Majangwa, and get away from this detestable old ... yes, you are old, Kalekezi, an old, old, old man. And how do you think you're going to live now with no one to look after you? Next time you lie under that blanket you'll be really dead and with none to be sorry for you either.

Exit with MAJANGWA, *drumming.* KAZUNGU *begins to slink out too but* KALEKEZI *stops him.*

KALEKEZI: Sit down and take a little of the bottle with me.

KAZUNGU: I am thirsty. What with the fear of death you put on me and driving cattle all day, I'm very thirsty.

KALEKEZI: I intended to beat you hard, but you're a quiet man. Here. (*Pours two cups of waragi and hands one to* KAZUNGU.)

KAZUNGU: Thank you and may you have a long and quiet life and good health with it.

Curtain

Third Party Insurance

PETER KINYANJUI

Characters

JACOB   A school teacher
SALOME
WILLIE   An Army Corporal

> JACOB *is discovered on a tree-stump impatiently awaiting someone's arrival. From time to time he looks at his watch and dusts his clothes.* SALOME *enters hurriedly.*

JACOB: Hello! Dear Sally. I thought you would never come.

SALOME (*unapologetically*): Sorry to keep you waiting, but I had a good reason for being late.

JACOB: What reason, my dear?

SALOME (*opening her handbag and producing a letter*): This letter came as I was dressing up, and I had to stop everything in order to read it first.

JACOB (*displeased but tries to conceal it*): From whom is it, if I may ask?

SALOME (*throwing the envelope to him*): Guess from that.

JACOB: Hmm! From Willie, eh? How is he getting on in the army?

> SALOME *is so much absorbed in the letter that she does not answer immediately.*

SALOME (*with a start*): What did you ask?

JACOB: How far has he gone in his army career?

SALOME: Oh, he is now a . . . I forget what he calls it . . . (*She consults the letter.*) Yes, here it is. He is now a Corporal.

JACOB (*sneering*): I see . . . What else does he say?

SALOME: So many things.

JACOB: The old stuff and nonsense about the army.

SALOME: Oh, no! This is a very important and special letter.

JACOB: Important and special?

SALOME (*excited*): And he says he's coming home to-morrow. I shall be going to meet him at the station.

JACOB: But you have a date with me to go out for a picnic.

SALOME: That! We shall go out another day, but not to-morrow. Certainly not to-morrow.

JACOB: But why? How can you change your mind so suddenly? Tell me, Salome. What do you find in this man that attracts you? I thought you were sensible enough to realize what type of husband he would make. You don't know these army people. And one day you will regret it.

SALOME: Leave me alone. You don't know how I regret that I came. Suppose someone were to find us here together, what would they say?

JACOB: They would say that they have never known two people better suited to each other than you and me.

SALOME: And how mistaken they would be!

JACOB: Salome, do you know that I've often dreamt that you were my wife and a mother to my children. I've often pictured you and me walking about in this wood, not as man and woman, but as husband and wife. Let me read you a little poem I wrote when I woke up from one of such dreams (*produces his notebook and reads*) . . .

> Sally, often have I dreamt of you as my dear wife
> And a mother to my ten children;
> Often have I seen visions of you and me
> Enjoying the cool evening breeze of these very woods,
> Walking in the bliss of holy matrimony . . .

SALOME: No, Jacob, don't waste your breath. My mind is made up. I have never imagined you as my husband or a father to my children.

JACOB: And you have been mad enough to picture Willie as such a man?

SALOME: At least he is the one who comes nearest to my ideas of an ideal husband. In him I find strength, courage, power, charm ... O my Willie! (*Produces Willie's photograph, kisses it and presses it to her breasts, then after a sigh ...*) My wandering boy, when will you settle down at home with me?

JACOB: Listen to me Salome. You are just behaving like a foolish school-girl, and you will regret it if you marry this man. Take advice from wiser people.

SALOME (*defiantly*): *You* are a wise man, Jacob. *I* am only a foolish girl. A wise man like you does not want a foolish girl like me for a wife, does he?

JACOB: Have you never read, my dear, what Rudyard Kipling once said? (*Opens his notebook and clears his throat.*) 'The silliest woman can manage a clever man; but it needs a very clever woman to manage a fool.'

SALOME (*not impressed*): I wish Willie were here to hear you call him a fool.

JACOB: Yes, I repeat he is a fool. And a fool and his property are soon parted, I warn you.

SALOME: Enough of your preaching. Didn't I tell you that I have made up my mind? Hear this with both your ears. I shall have no child by any man except Willie. Of all the sons of Adam I've met, he is the one who is good enough to be the father of my children. Let him come to-morrow and—oh, the thought of it ...

JACOB: He may never come home. Why don't you accept me and you will be assured of a lasting and happy marriage? (*Walks towards her with outstretched arms.*)

Someone is heard whistling a popular tune off stage as he approaches.

E

SALOME (*with a start*): Listen! Someone is coming this way. (*Goes to look.*) It's Willie, God help us! He's coming up this way. Oh! Jacob, what shall we do?

JACOB (*confused*): Let's hide behind that bush.

SALOME: No, you pretend to be collecting leaves for your next nature study lesson, and I'll hide myself. (*She conceals herself.*)

Enter WILLIE, marching to his tune. He is a robust young man, proud of his profession.

WILLIE: Hai! Mwalimu Jacob. What are you doing in the woods alone?

JACOB: Oh! It's you, Corporal Willie. It's nice to see you.

WILLIE (*looking down at his stripes*): It's amazing how news circulates. It was only a week ago . . .

JACOB: I heard it from Salome. She also told me that you were due to arrive to-morrow.

WILLIE (*threateningly*): O! When did you see her last?

JACOB (*suddenly alarmed, but pretending to be casual*): It was the day before yesterday . . . I think. Yes, I remember now because I had a puncture in the rear tyre of my bicycle.

WILLIE: Has she been kicking around with boys very much?

JACOB (*pretending not to understand*): My bicycle? Oh, no, I'm the only person who rides her.

WILLIE: Idiot! I'm not asking about your damn bike. I'm asking about Salome! And you tell me that you are the only person who . . .

JACOB: Oh! I'm sorry. I thought you were talking about my bike. Oh, you meant Salome? Ah, she is one of the few good girls we have in the village. I don't think I've ever seen her with a boy.

WILLIE *notices* SALOME's *handbag lying nearby. Smiles broadly and coughs.*

WILLIE: Has it become men's fashion to carry handbags these days?

JACOB: O! Eh . . . It was given me by Salome to take to her home.

WILLIE: Hmm! I have a hunch that something is going on behind my back. Has she come to trust you so much that she even entrusts her handbag to your safekeeping?

JACOB: No, Willie, you are mistaken. Nothing has been passing between Salome and me. I treat her just as I would my sister.

WILLIE: One thing I want to make quite clear to you before I get angry and lose my power of reasoning. It's this. I would never share a woman with you. Do you hear? Never! My valour won't allow.

JACOB: Neither would I. My education wouldn't allow.

WILLIE: I've been through fire and water while you have been wasting your time in the village.

JACOB: And I've been through books of learning while you have been wasting your time in the army.

WILLIE: Don't echo me, you parrot. Shut that mouth if you don't want to spit out those teeth.

JACOB: You shut your mouth first.

WILLIE: How dare you! Ruffian, bush man, damn fool, idiot . . .

JACOB: Have you finished? If I'm all those, I don't know what to call you.

WILLIE: By God! I'm not used to being spoken to like this. Never!

JACOB: Nor am I.

WILLIE (*enraged. Rushes at* JACOB): O stupid fool! Goddamit.

A blow aimed at JACOB *misses him.* SALOME *rushes out of hiding, screaming, and holds* WILLIE's *hands.*

SALOME: Stop, Willie. Stop! Forgive him please . . .

WILLIE (*letting* JACOB's *hand go*): Aha! You tried to save her by hiding her. Thank her for she has saved your life.

SALOME: Willie! What are you doing here? You said you would come to-morrow.

WILLIE: Husbands come when their wives least expect them.

SALOME: Your talking about husbands and wives reminds me of something I wanted to tell you on your arrival.

WILLIE: Don't try to be cunning. I have seen so much of this life especially where women are concerned. I can guess what you have been doing during my absence. I could read your mind even as you were hiding behind that bush.

SALOME: But you did not know I was there.

WILLIE: Let me tell you, this nose has been trained to smell human beings hiding behind the thickest bush. And when those beings happen to be of the female type . . .

SALOME: Why won't you listen to the more important things that I'm about to tell you instead of . . . of . . .

WILLIE: Jacob, what has been going on between you and this woman? Now, hear me. I'm not going to share this woman with you. And if you think you are good enough to rival me, you will have to prove it within this triangle. (*He draws a triangle on the ground with a stick.*)

JACOB: Willie, I've never had a single fight over a woman, and this is not going to be my first.

WILLIE: And I've never had a single woman without a fight and this is not going to be my first. Man, I've seen the world. How and where do you think I received this scar? (*Reveals the scar on his thigh.*)

JACOB: Indeed! It's triangular in shape.

SALOME: Tell us about it. Tell us about your adventures, Willie.

WILLIE: Oh! Are you still there? Don't forget I have a bone to pick with you too. You will tell me all about your adventures.

SALOME: Tell me yours first.

WILLIE: Bush girl. My stories would not interest you at all. They are all about the three W's.

SALOME (*interested*): The three what?

WILLIE: W's. Don't you know the . . . the . . . 23rd letter of the alphabet?

SALOME: I don't understand.

WILLIE: How can you? The three W's comprise what we call the Great Triangle.

SALOME: Triangle?

WILLIE: Yes, Triangle. But don't go on repeating words after me. I hate parrots. Yes. As I was saying, in the army, we have what we call the 3, 4, 5 Triangle.

SALOME: 3, 4, 5 Triangle?

WILLIE: I told you not to be a parrot. 3 stands for W-A-R.

He takes three paces as he speaks along one side of his triangle.

SALOME: War.

WILLIE (*Taking four paces along another side*): 4 for W-I-N-E.

SALOME: Wine.

WILLIE (*Taking five paces back to where he started*): And 5 for W-O-M-E-N.

SALOME (*giggling*): Women.

JACOB: I see you are engaged in some interesting mathematics. It was only last week when I was teaching my pupils the Pythagoras Theorem and . . .

WILLIE: Away with your Pythagoras Theorem. (*Putting an arm round* SALOME.) *This* is *my* theorem.

JACOB (*sitting down*): And since yours is a 3, 4, 5 Triangle, then it must be a right-angled triangle.

WILLIE: It will be a right-angled triangle provided that you get the things in their right order. Take, for example, Wine plus Women. This will always lead to War.

JACOB (*writes in his notebook and murmurs to himself*): Wine plus Women equals War. War plus Women equals . . . (*Scratches his head.* WILLIE *and* SOLOME *exchange glances.*)

WILLIE: Ha! This world of pen and paper. Must you write everything down in order to remember? Man, I keep a hundred dates with the 3 W's and, damn me, if I've ever forgotten one of them. And I keep no diary.

JACOB (*with new enthusiasm*): It is amazing Willie, this problem of triangularity. Let's face it. Take our case here for example. Look at the formation in which we are standing.

WILLIE: Triangular, you mean?

JACOB: Yes. Do you think there will ever be peace between two men and one woman? Or two women and one man for that matter? It has always been the universal triangle of sex.

SALOME: You men are jealous. Why doesn't one withdraw and try his luck elsewhere?

WILLIE: I'll answer you by a question. You may have Stephen here in love with say, Elizabeth. Don't we always find a Miss X hovering in the background? Stephen, Elizabeth, X . . . SEX.

JACOB: It is indeed a world of triangularities.

SALOME: It has been right from the beginning. Adam and Eve were at peace until the unknown third party came between them.

JACOB: And how difficult it is to escape this third party, however much we insure ourselves against him. Why has no one ever thought of introducing a kind of third party insurance policy? Don't you think it would place a guarantee for fidelity between wives and husbands? If ever I marry, I will insure my wife against this ever-present unknown 'third-party'.

SALOME: If ever I get a husband I shall insure him against all other females.

WILLIE: And what would you insure a soldier like me against? War, wine or women?

SALOME: Women, of course.

WILLIE: Why?

SALOME: Because they are my worst enemies as far as you are concerned.

WILLIE: As far as I am concerned women are an essential part of the whole game of life.

SALOME (drawing him aside): Willie, it's high time you started planning for our future. I've been anxiously waiting for your arrival because . . . because . . . there is something I've got to tell you.

WILLIE: Out with it and say it hot.

SALOME: Yes, if only you would stop interrupting me. You know we've been friends for a long time now. I've refused other men's offers because of you. We've got to start thinking seriously of settling down together. Times have changed. Things are not as they used to be—if you catch my meaning.

WILLIE: I don't, I'm afraid.

She whispers in his ear.

WILLIE: What?

SALOME: Yes, it's true.

WILLIE: You mean . . .? My Gawd! Do you know what you're saying?

SALOME: Yes. I'm quite certain it's you. It can't be anyone else.

WILLIE (*laughing*): Woman, you don't know what you're saying. Do you think this is the first time I've heard such a story? Can you imagine me as a husband and a father? I swear you're crazy if you think I'm cut out for such a life. (*He prepares to leave.*)

SALOME: But Willie! (*She bursts into tears.*) What shall I do? You know . . . you . . .

WILLIE: Do you ask me that? Send him to the army when he grows up. And suppose it's a girl? Oh well, more trouble and bother for men. What a world! (*Exits whistling.*)

SALOME (*weeping*): What shall I do?

JACOB: What does he mean? Is the fellow mad?

SALOME (*pulling herself together*): Jacob, I have to tell you this. I'm going to have a baby.

JACOB: Going to have a baby? Why that's nothing to cry about. That's marvellous!

SALOME (*wailing*): Yes, but it's Willie's baby.

JACOB: Oh, oh, I see.

SALOME: But Jacob, Willie doesn't want me now.

JACOB: What? Willie doesn't want to marry you? Well then that's all right. It's still marvellous.

SALOME: But what shall I do?

JACOB: Why, marry me, of course.

SALOME: But will you still have me?

JACOB: Salome, really, what kind of man do you think I am? Why should I love you any less now than before? No fear of that, my dear. I love you for what you are to me. Forget that monster of a soldier. He was picked up by the roadside. Salome, will you marry me?

SALOME: And the child?

JACOB: The child will be fine. No one need ever know the truth. It will remain a secret between you and me. Will you have me?

SALOME: Oh, what a fool I've been. Of course, I'll marry you, Jacob. I do love you. And I promise that I'll always be true to you.

JACOB: I believe you, Salome. But just in case you ever are tempted to look at another soldier, I think your baby will be the best kind of third party insurance in the end.

Curtain

Bones

A sketch written in Swahili and translated by

SADRU KASSAM

Characters

THE BUTCHER
DONGO   A health inspector
KANUBHAI   A Hindu trader
A WOMAN ⎫
A GIRL ⎭ customers

Scene:
   A butcher's shop. A sign reads: 'SALEH BIN AWADH,
   The Big Butcher, P.O. MAJI MOTO, Coast Region'. On one
   wall is a painting of a bull, and on another a picture of the BUTCHER
   slaughtering another bull. There are notices reading: *'FRASH*
   MEAT' and 'WEL-COME'.

Note:
   It is intended that each scene shall open with an extended mime by
   the BUTCHER, *which can be developed from the outlines in the stage*
   directions.

Scene 1

The shop is tolerably clean and tidy. The BUTCHER *wears an almost*
white coat and his hair is combed. He sings as he arranges his meat

to conceal its shortcomings. A joint tumbles to the ground: he looks to see if anyone is around, then picks it up and brushes it before replacing it, clean side upwards. He spits and scratches himself vigorously. He starts dividing some meat into smaller sections with a large knife, swinging the blade dangerously. At length he cuts himself, shrieks, prances around, tends his bleeding finger, wipes the blood off on a piece of meat and sucks the wound. The WOMAN *is heard singing as she approaches. She enters, wearing a khanga.*

WOMAN: Eee, banakuba! How are you?

BUTCHER: Me? Very well, mama, very well. You want meat?

WOMAN: Yes, banakuba, I want meat. How's your meat? Is it good?

BUTCHER: Very good, mama. Good and fresh. Can't you see me in the picture there slaughtering a bull?

WOMAN: From what part will you give me?

BUTCHER: Any part you want, mama. Whatever you ask for, I'm here to serve you.

He sharpens his knife on his file.

WOMAN: I want some of that. I hope it's fresh.

BUTCHER: Completely fresh, mama: numberi one. How much do you want?

WOMAN: Aaaah! A shilling's worth only—unless you want to give me more on credit.

BUTCHER: No, no, no, not today.

The BUTCHER *cuts a small piece from the meat the* WOMAN *has chosen, and then begins to cut larger pieces from another joint.*

WOMAN: A-a-a-a, I want off that only.

BUTCHER: Yes, but you want good and fresh meat, isn't it? This is very good. See . . . excellent! Numberi one! I tell you.

WOMAN (*violently*): I *don't* want it.

BUTCHER: O.K. . . . your wish. Was it this one you wanted?

WOMAN: That's it. Now you know it.

He puts some meat on the scales, and is about to add several bones.

WOMAN: What's that you're doing there? I didn't ask for stones. I don't want them. Remove them at once.
BUTCHER: Mama, they aren't stones. They are very good bones with plenty of meat on them. See . . . excellent! Grade one!
WOMAN: And what am I to do with bones? I'm not a dog.

He finishes weighing the meat and wraps it. The WOMAN *takes out a small pouch and offers money which she draws back as the* BUTCHER *tries to snatch it, so that he pitches across his counter before she gives it to him.*

BUTCHER: Here it is, mama, your meat.
WOMAN: And here's your money . . . unless you don't want it.
BUTCHER: Eh, why not? Thank you, mama, thank you very much. God help you.
WOMAN: O.K., banakuba, goodbye.

A GIRL *enters, dressed in a dirty, tattered frock and carrying a kikapu.*

GIRL: Get me half a pound of meat, please. Nice—like you!

As the WOMAN *is going out she bumps into* DONGO *as he enters.*

DONGO: Good morning, mama.
WOMAN: Good morning, brother.
DONGO: What's the quarrel with the butcher?
WOMAN: Aaaa, nothing.
DONGO: Weren't you complaining of ill-treatment? I heard you shouting.
WOMAN: No, no, no. I was just joking with him. That butcher is a very nice man, you know.
DONGO: I see. O.K. Goodbye.
WOMAN: Goodbye. (*Exit.*)
GIRL: Give me very good meat, and no bones, please.

BUTCHER: No, no, no. No bones. Just a little one for your father.

GIRL: No. My father has no teeth.

BUTCHER: Oh, I see. (DONGO *has been clearing his throat loudly to attract the* BUTCHER'S *attention.*) Dongo, Mr Dongo! Just come over here, please. I'm delighted to see you. How are you?

DONGO: Excellent, thank you. And you?

BUTCHER: Aaaa, not well at all, because you know you still haven't endorsed my trading licence. Please do it just now. Only a week is left before the closing date.

DONGO *stands as if ready to receive a gift. He looks away, pauses, then looks back at his hand as if surprised to see it empty.*

DONGO: Your trading licence? Hasn't anyone taught you how to get it? (*The* BUTCHER *shakes his head.*) Just look at your shop! (DONGO *sweeps a pile of scraps from the counter onto the floor.*) See, the whole floor is littered with scraps and bones. When did you last sweep it? (DONGO *wipes his hands, now covered in blood from the meat, on the* BUTCHER'S *apron.*) And why is your apron so dirty? Where is your file? (DONGO *takes the file and breaks it in two.*) Why is it broken? (*He runs his hands through the* BUTCHER'S *hair, ruffling it.*) And why have you not combed your hair? Who made you a big butcher? Look, you must get things in order before pestering me to endorse your licence. Do you understand that?

BUTCHER: I . . . I . . . I'm sorry. I didn't know about these things. If . . . if you return next week, I promise everything will be in order. But please, I must have the licence endorsed by next Monday.

DONGO: That's your business. I'm warning you, if everything is not ready by next week, you won't get your licence, is that clear?

BUTCHER: Yes, yes. Everything will be in order next week. I promise.

DONGO: Your business. (*Exit.*)

GIRL: Come on, where's my meat?

BUTCHER: Oh, dear, yes. I'm sorry. I won't be a minute. Here
it is. (*She exits. The* BUTCHER *surveys his shop in despair.*) What's
to be done? And that girl, she didn't pay me. Which way did
she go? Too late: she's made off. (*Enter* KANUBHAI, *a Hindu
trader, in dhoti and cap. He holds his nose in disgust as he passes
the* BUTCHER'S *shop.*) Kanubhai! Oh, Kanubhai! Just come
over here please, quick.

KANUBHAI: Come near your stinking meat? No, no, no, never!

BUTCHER: Ah, this old man! (*He comes from his shop and crosses to*
KANUBHAI.) Kanubhai, please help me. You know that
health inspector, he's refusing to endorse my trading licence.
I whitewashed my shop and I bought a new apron, but still
he comes and asks me why my shop's dirty, and why my hair
is not stylishly done, and what not. What am I to do?

KANUBHAI: That man! I know him. He's a dog. He's hungry.

BUTCHER: Hungry?

KANUBHAI: Yes, hungry. He wants some bones. (*He pretends to
snarl.*)

BUTCHER: Bones?

KANUBHAI: Yes, bones. You still don't understand? (*He takes
out some coins, jingles them, and pretends to eat them, snarling as he
does so.*) He wants bones, bones!

BUTCHER: Oh, bones, bones! Yes, I see, he wants some bones.

As KANUBHAI *exits, the* BUTCHER *leaps joyfully into the air,
claps his hands, and returns purposefully to his shop.*

Scene 2

The same scene a week later. The floor is littered with rubbish. The BUTCHER's *apron is filthy. Rusty knives and broken implements lie around.*

ANNOUNCER: The same scene. One week later.

The BUTCHER *stretches, yawns, scratches himself, spits on the floor, kicks at the rubbish. Enter* DONGO; *he coughs. The* BUTCHER *works at his counter, pretending not to have seen* DONGO, *who strolls with exaggerated casualness up to the shop. The* BUTCHER *looks up, pretending surprise.*

BUTCHER: Oh, Dongo! Good morning. How are you?

DONGO: Mmm! Not so well.

BUTCHER: Not well? I'm very sorry. Anyway, I hope you've come to endorse my licence.

DONGO: Endorse your licence? Just like that? With such a dirty shop?

BUTCHER: Oh, by the way, Mr Dongo, I almost forgot: I have something for you. I thought you might like a few bones to take home.

The BUTCHER *hands* DONGO *a small package.*

DONGO: Bones? Bones? What should I want with bones? (*As he fumbles with the package, a couple of coins fall out. He chases after them, and then slips the package in his pocket.*) Oh, bones, bones! That's very thoughtful of you. They will come in very handy. (*He smiles broadly.*) Mr Awadh, your shop looks really clean today. See, no cobwebs, a clean scale, a new broom, a dustbin outside. It's the way we want it. Don't you worry about your hair. Come on, give me those forms. (*The* BUTCHER *hands him the forms.* DONGO *takes out a pen, goes to sign, but finds the nib is broken.*) Just lend me your pen, please. Something's gone wrong with mine.

BUTCHER: Certainly, certainly. I'm at your service.

The BUTCHER *hands over his pen, which* DONGO *examines admiringly.*

DONGO: Eh, you've bought a new pen. (*He finishes signing and slips the pen into his own pocket.*) Well that's done. Now you'll be all right. O.K., Mr Awadh, kwaheri.

BUTCHER: Thank you. Kwaheri, kwaheri.

DONGO: Kwaheri.

BUTCHER: Kwaheri.

DONGO *goes out and then returns for his hat, which he had put on the counter while signing.*

DONGO: Ah, my hat, there it is. Kwaheri, kwaheri.

BUTCHER: Kwaheri. (DONGO *goes out. The* BUTCHER *returns to his work. Enter the* WOMAN. *She surveys the shop, screws up her face, holds her nose, and walks past with her head in the air.*) Hello, mama! Good morning. (*She eyes him sourly.*) Aren't you coming to buy meat today?

WOMAN: Just look at your shop! And at yourself! Dirty and stinking! I'm not going to buy meat from you any more. I'm going to the next butcher, to a cleaner shop. (*Exit.*)

BUTCHER: But mama, mama, I have my licence. Listen. (*He reads.*) 'Certified clean and fit to sell meat for human consumption.' Mama! Mama!

Curtain

The Famine

A Luganda fable dramatized in the vernacular and translated by

JOSEPH MUKASA-BALIKUDDEMBE

Characters

KATO
NNANKYA   his wife

Scene
   On a foot-path leading to a village; then in the house of KATO *and* NNANKYA.

Time   Late afternoon.

   The opening scene on the foot-path may be played in front of the curtain. As the play opens, KATO *has just killed a rat.*

KATO: Ha! If rats were eatable, this would make a very delicious dish ... But ... wait a minute ... My hunting has been fruitless, and this means another bowlful of green vegetables for supper. I can't go on eating weeds for weeks just because my wife preserves bananas for visitors. (*Pause.*) This rat will do the trick. (*He ties the rat on his left leg.*) Now, when she sees me limping, she will think I have a wound on my leg. And one of those bunches of matoke she is hoarding must be cooked today. (*Exit.*)

The scene changes to the house. Enter NNANKYA. *She sits on a mat and starts sorting vegetables.*

NNANKYA: Good gracious! I am getting tired of having to walk miles to fetch these wild leaves. The hunters must learn how to trap those bushbucks properly, or we shall soon starve to death.

KATO, *pretending to be ill, calls from the doorway.*

KATO: Nnankya . . . Nnankya. Are you in?

He limps into the room.

NNANKYA: Yes, but I was beginning to get worried . . .
KATO: We hunted far away today, and you can see for yourself why I could not walk very fast. The antelope we had trapped jumped out of the net, and we ran after it; one of our friends, coming from the side, threw his spear, but missed the animal, and as I was trying to avoid the flying blade, a large thorn caught me here on the leg and tore out a piece of flesh. Thus the chase was abandoned; my companions found me herbs to tie on the wound, and carried me on their shoulders up to the junction leading to our courtyard. I think I must go to bed immediately: I feel feverish.

He rises and limps dramatically towards the bed.

NNANKYA: I'm sorry about this accident, dear. I wish you had listened to me when I advised you not to go hunting today.

She rises to bring him a bowl of vegetables.

KATO: But, my dear, how can you expect me to stay away from hunting when food is so scarce? Anyway, I think a piece of hunted meat would occasionally break the monotony of wild leaves.
NNANKYA: I failed to find any wild yams for lunch, but this will be better than an empty stomach.

She kneels by the bed. He tastes a mouthful from the bowl and then spits it out.

KATO: E-e, Nnankya, this smells like medicine. Please take it away.

He settles down in the bed.

NNANKYA: You certainly can't sleep with an empty stomach as if you were a widower or bachelor. Let me cook that small cluster of bananas I had preserved for visitors. But I have no ground-nuts: you don't mind that, do you?

KATO: Well, if we can't find ground-nuts, we can do without them. Just add a bit of salt, that's all. (*She exits.*) This stingy woman! Keeping food for visitors as if I had lost my appetite for matoke. Now I know the trick. If I must be ill in order to deserve those bananas, I shall remain in bed until they are all finished. She's not going to starve me by keeping food for visitors who never come.

He pretends to sleep. NNANKYA *enters with a bunch of bananas which she leaves on the mat, and a basket which she takes to the bed.*

NNANKYA: Kato, are you fast asleep?

KATO: N-N-No-oo! I was just dreaming about that antelope I was chasing in the forest.

NNANKYA: Sit up, now, and eat a little; you must not sleep with nothing in your stomach.

KATO *sits up, and eats the food from the basket ravenously.*

KATO: Thanks. This is certainly better than nothing.

Exit NNANKYA. KATO *falls asleep and snores.* NNANKYA *re-enters and finds* KATO *sleeping.*

NNANKYA: I must attend to his wound. But . . . it might be so painful that he will kick and make it worse. I know: I'll tie him down to the bed with this rope and then unbind his leg. (*She does so.*)

KATO: Nnankya, leave the wound alone. I have already treated it with herbs. What are you doing? You're hurting me.

He attempts to get free without success. NNANKYA *unties the binding and discovers the dead rat.*

NNANKYA: Woo-oo-oo! You greedy, impossible husband! Why did you deceive me thus? This is unbearable! I am fed up with your pranks.

She throws the rat in KATO's *face and angrily begins to collect her clothes.* KATO *continues to wriggle vainly under the rope.*

NNANKYA: Goodbye. I shall not return until you are cured of your insatiable greed. You can finish up that remaining bunch of bananas. (*She exits.*)

KATO (*struggling free*): Nnankya! Nnankya! The woman has gone. This is shameful. She will broadcast the incident all over the village. I won't stand it.

He angrily rolls up his bedding and puts it on the mat.

I won't allow her to shame me in my own house. I shall settle in a foreign land.

He ties his spear, his big knife and his stick onto the bundle with the rope.

For the shame she is bringing on me, her lawful husband, let the spirits of her faithfully married grandmothers torment her to her dying day.

He sets the bundle on his head and is about to exit, but stops and looks back at the bunch of bananas. He goes and picks it up, looks at it critically, puts it on top of his bundle and goes out.

Curtain

The Mirror

A Runyoro/Rutoro fable dramatized in the vernacular and translated by

JOSEPH MUKASA-BALIKUDDEMBE

Characters
BAMUROGA
KABULEETA   his wife
ZAHURA   their neighbour

Scene: BAMUROGA's *hut in a remote village.*

Time: *Early twentieth century. Morning.*

> *A simple curtain partitions off a bed from the rest of the room, and for the moment conceals a mirror hanging on the wall. As the play opens,* BAMUROGA *is clambering out of this bed. He washes his face in a basin of water. He dries himself before the mirror; closes the curtain; yawns; and shakes his head.*

BAMUROGA: Ohooo . . . I have an impossible woman. I gave her just one day to go and see her parents and she multiplies that by five. She never remembers that my bananas are ready for the brewing of beer. I buy a new mirror, the first in the village, as a surprise for her, but she never thinks of me. If her father is seriously ill, I can't see why they don't send me a message. Anyway, I shall wait no longer for her help. I'll get everything ready, and then she will have to do the rest alone. (*He sneezes.*) Well, if she doesn't return soon, I will have to find someone to take her place.

He picks up a large knife, goes to the food baskets, takes a piece of cassava, and goes out eating. KABULEETA *enters with a bundle of working clothes. She looks into the cooking pots, and then changes into the clothes she has been carrying.*

KABULEETA: Good. That's done. I don't know what my man will say about my staying away so long. I must prepare his lunch early to stop him from finding an excuse for a quarrel.

She bundles her travelling clothes together and carries them to the bed. As she pulls the curtain she sees her own reflection in the mirror and jumps back, furious.

So, there's another woman in the house. My husband has found someone to replace me in my absence, has he? I'll soon tell her what I think of her. (*She addresses her own reflection.*) I can see that you have assumed complete authority in this house. Let me warn you beforehand that I shall not cook under the same roof as a sneaking harlot. You see these cups, these plates, these pots? Well, I bought them with my own money from my mother, and I shall take them back with me. You will have to buy your own.

As she is furiously collecting her possessions together, a mug accidentally drops to the floor. In a rage, she throws everything down again.

I have laboured and cooked for this dress. You, too, will have to sweat before you can earn one like it.

She tears the dress and throws the rags on the floor. Then she kneels down and ties the cups and pots onto her bundle. BAMUROGA *enters and puts his big knife in a corner.*

BAMUROGA: Darling, how is father? Why don't you answer? And what is all this luggage for? Has someone been taken to hospital? Please tell me. Darling, are you angry about something.

KABULEETA: I am no more a darling of yours. That endearment has now got a new owner.

BAMUROGA: You don't usually speak in such a manner. What kind of words are these?

KABULEETA: You will have to ask the woman whom you find to be a better wife than me.

BAMUROGA: Kabuleeta, why do you always suspect me of being unfaithful to you? How many times have you seen me running after other women?

KABULEETA: It is no use putting on airs now. I have caught you in the act. This time you will have your meals cooked by your concubine.

BAMUROGA: Kabuleeta, are you looking for a quarrel? You will force me to beat you.

KABULEETA: Whether you beat me or not, I know you have been flirting with other women.

BAMUROGA: I am tired of your false accusations. This time I'll show you that I mean what I say.

He picks up a stick and intercepts her as she rushes for the door. He grabs her and pushes her backwards, brandishing the stick as he does so. She drops her bundle as she struggles and yells.

KABULEETA: Wala-la-la-aa! Help! Murder! Help! Zahura-a-a! Help! I am lost! Murder! Help! Wala-la-la-aa!

BAMUROGA: Stop shouting or I will knock your teeth out.

Enter ZAHURA. *He grabs* BAMUROGA's *arm.*

ZAHURA: Stop it, Bamuroga. Stop! Don't kill your wife.

BAMUROGA *releases* KABULEETA *and pushes her back. She staggers and begins to sob.*

BAMUROGA: Zahura, if you were a stranger in this house, I wouldn't stand for your interruption. That woman is getting too big for her shoes. When I give her permission to go and see her father for a day, she returns after five days, and then tries to cover up her own faults by accusing me of being unfaithful. She hasn't even greeted me yet, or told me a word about her sick father. I won't swallow this any longer. So she can be thankful for your arrival: it was in the nick of time for her. (*He throws the stick down.*)

ZAHURA: Kabuleeta!

KABULEETA (*drying her eyes*): Ye-e-es.

ZAHURA: Are you hurt?

KABULEETA: N-no. B-but he would have beaten me if you had not arrived.

ZAHURA: That deafening alarm made me run as if murder had broken out all over the village. Come now, forgive and forget this quarrel. Stay in your house and cook for your husband.

KABULEETA: You can say what you like, but I will not cook with a concubine under the same roof. I had offers from plenty of other men when he married me.

ZAHURA: My friend, this second woman of yours is now breaking your home.

BAMUROGA: If she believes that I have another woman, let her try to prove it.

KABULEETA: Come and see for yourself. (*She beckons* ZAHURA *towards the partition, draws the curtain, and reveals her own image in the mirror.*) Look at her goggle eyes. You shameless woman! How dare you come here and try to steal my man!

ZAHURA: Eeh, Bamuroga, haven't you introduced your wife to this mirror yet?

BAMUROGA: No, I haven't had a chance. The day I bought it, I arrived home at night; and I didn't see any point in waking her up; and the following day she left early to see her parents, while I was still in bed.

ZAHURA: I would never have dreamt that a mere looking-glass could threaten to break a marriage. Now that this quarrel is

over, I must go and get on with my work, and leave you two
to make it up between you. Bye bye. (*Exit.*)

BAMUROGA: My dear, I really thought you must have had some
good reason for suspecting me so bitterly. This is simply a
mirror so that we can see ourselves while we are dressing.
Now, come and look for yourself. Don't be afraid. There is
no one else there. You see, darling, it was your own reflection you mistook for a rival. So there is no need to get
jealous. You are the only queen in this house. I have no
other.

KABULEETA *stares into the mirror; makes gestures, and then faces
at herself; laughs, delighted; and then looks into* BAMUROGA'*s eyes.*

KABULEETA: Darling, forgive me. I really thought I had lost
your love.

Curtain

Note to Producers

A producer's job is creative; and every producer will interpret the text of a play somewhat differently, according to his own reaction to it and the individual qualities of the members of his cast. We feel very strongly, therefore, that acting editions of plays should include neither groundplans of the setting; nor details of the actors' movements; nor any lighting plan. Such technical instructions would probably irritate the experienced producer, who will know that his job is to present a single, meaningful version of the drama, not a hotch-potch of other people's versions; and, worse still, might confuse the inexperienced producer and undermine his confidence in his own ability to make decisions on these matters; whereas learning to make such decisions, in consultation with technical advisers and actors, is the first essential in mastering the art of production. We do not presume, for this reason, to give any detailed advice on how to present the plays in this book; we hope, instead, only to touch on one or two principles with which some producers may not be very familiar. In other words, we think it is possible usefully to propose a few questions that producers might well ask themselves, but not to indicate how they ought to answer them.

Actors for whom English is a second language will find it very helpful to receive some advice from a producer on the difference in stress and intonation between English and their mother tongues. English makes a very marked contrast between stressed and unstressed syllables: and so, if too little emphasis is given to English stresses, English speech will be at best dull, and at worst incomprehensible. Girls in particular may need to realize that in speaking English forcefully they will not be giving the same impression as if they spoke their own language with equal energy; but rather that this kind of vigour is essential to drama in English.

One of the most important aspects of production, yet one which is all too seldom taken into consideration by amateurs, is pace. Many carefully prepared performances are spoilt by dragging on from beginning to end at the same speed. A producer will probably want to determine what sections a play falls into; and then where the climax of each section comes. There are climaxes of action, such as Dehota's struggle to stop the fortune-tellers running away in *Born To Die*; or of emotion such as the revelation of the real love between the King and Nannono in *The Secret*; or of ideas, as in the argument in *Undesignated*; though these are not, of course, watertight categories. Then the producer will have to decide which are the most important climaxes in the play; and ensure that dramatic excitement really does reach a peak at the intended moment, and comes up to smaller peaks at other chosen points. In between there may be quieter, slower passages. Actors must be made to realize that they cannot create a sense of speed by gabbling their words. What is needed is the appearance of speed, and this is created by the intensity of the acting and the building up of excitement in the production.

The importance of silences and pauses must also be borne in mind. Very important moments may best be underlined by quietness—the arrival of the police at the end of *Born To Die* or the throwing down of the blood-stained bead in *The Exodus*.

Several of the plays in this book are in more than one scene; and yet an interruption in a one-act drama may break its back and lose all the dramatic power that has been built up in the first scene. Producers will want to ask themselves whether the curtain need really be dropped, or whether only a slight pause is required: certainly *The Exodus* and *Bones* have frequently been performed with no more than a few objects being moved, in full view of the audience, to change the scene, and an announcer proclaiming the passing of time. If it is decided that the curtain must be closed, then the time interval will want to be restricted to a matter of seconds, not minutes.

There is an apparently small technical point which often, in fact, proves to be of crucial importance, especially in producing African plays. Since rehearsals are normally conducted in an empty hall or open space, it is easy for inexperienced producers to forget how difficult it will be once a large audience has gathered for the spectators to see any action which involves characters lying or sitting on the floor of the stage (unless one is lucky enough to be working in a theatre with sloped seating). In plays with a village setting it may seem only too natural for quite long conversations to be conducted in a squatting position; while death agonies may appear to require an actor to grovel on the ground; but in planning dramatic movements one must always remember that it is perilous to allow important figures to sink out of sight of a large section of the audience for any significant length of time; and considerable ingenuity may be needed to avoid such a situation.

When actors have long speeches, as they do in many of these plays, they will no doubt work on them in great detail with the producer, so that great variety can be introduced in speed, manner and effect. The slightest movement or gesture may impress the audience very deeply in such a passage if the performance is properly controlled. It may well be that, as rehearsals proceed, actor and producer develop quite different ideas about the characterization of a part. In such a case neither should attempt simply to override the views of the other. A performer must have the chance to develop a role in terms of his own abilities and attitudes but these must be adapted, as far as is humanly possible, to fit into a larger pattern, a unified interpretation of the play, which can be controlled only be the producer.

Finally, the producer will want at the very outset to consider the style in which he plans to produce the play. Perhaps an extremely realistic mode will be employed: *Undesignated* may well require such treatment. In *The Exodus* a more epic manner is possible, with carefully, and perhaps even symmetrically, posed groupings at certain points—notably at the very formal conclusion, when Labongo and Gipir cross their spears and then separate for ever. *Of Malice and Men* and *The Trick* offer a wide range of possible interpretations.

But on all these matters the producer must make considered choices, which will probably have been discussed with the players, remembering that all final decisions rest with the one person in charge. He or (she) must try to understand the wide range of issues on which the producer has to exercise careful judgement, reaching conclusions and then rehearsing to put them into practice with one overall purpose in mind—that the play as a whole shall have the appropriate impact on the audience.

Notes on the Authors

Tom Omara

Born in 1946, Tom Omara is a Ugandan, was educated in Lira and at King's College Budo, where he excelled in debating and play-writing, taking part in several school productions. He also won boxing trophies.

Sam Tulya-Muhika

Born in Kabale, Uganda. Makerere University College Maths (honours) graduate. Has had several short stories broadcast and some are to be published. Shortly going to Britain for post-graduate Maths. Hopes to use all possible language to express all possible life.

A. S. Bukenya

Born in 1944 at Masaka, Uganda. After secondary school in Kampala, he went to the University College, Dar es Salaam, Tanzania, where he is now doing his final year B.A. in Literature, and Language and Linguistics.

Joseph Mukasa-Balikuddembe

B.A. Honours (English), University of East Africa. Now Teaching on the Diploma in Drama Course at Makerere University College. Hoping to do research in Vernacular Drama in East Africa and to continue post-graduate work overseas.

Ganesh Bagchi

Born in 1924 and now his work is published for the first time. He writes 'Between these two events I worked in Uganda for twelve years as a teacher and wrote, produced and acted in several plays.'

Miles Lee, F.R.S.A.

Programme Organizer Features and Drama, Radio Uganda; was the producer for the Uganda Government's Heart Beat of Africa Troupe during 1964 and 1965. Before the war was Stage Director at the Birmingham Repertory Theatre. After six years' war service with the R.A.F. became Adviser to the Scottish Community Drama Association. Founded the Belgrave Mews Puppet Theatre, Edinburgh, in 1951. Free-lance producer for B.B.C. and Commercial Television as well as producing films for C.O.I. Outside lecturer to Moray House Teacher Training College, Edinburgh, as well as to the Overseas Visual Aid Centre, London. Mission to India 1958–60 as UNESCO Theatre expert to establish the Indian National Drama School and Asian Theatre Institute, New Dehli.

Sadru Kassam

Born 1941, Mombasa. Educated at The Aga Khan High School, Mombasa, and at Makerere from where he graduated in 1966 with Honours in English. From March 1967 to December 1967 taught at Harambee School near Embu. Since January this year, teaching English at Pumwani Secondary School, Nairobi.

Kuldip Sondhi

Forty-three years old, 'Engineer by training, writer by heart (or choice)' he says. He has twice won the Kenya Drama Festival Playwright's award. His most recent publication is *Bad Blood* in *African Writing Today*, published by Penguin. His hobbies are swimming and squash racquets.

Peter Kinyanjui

Comes from Kenya. He obtained his B.A. at Makerere in 1965 and later M.A. (Ed.) degree at Syracuse University. He is now Staff Tutor at the Institute of Adult Studies, University

College, Nairobi. He takes a keen interest in drama and broad-casting.

Erisa Kironde

Erisa Kironde is by conviction a school-teacher, presently working in a large electricity undertaking. He is promoter of Ugandan drama, imaginative writing and publishing, and a writer when life allows him to be.

David Cook

David Cook took both his degrees while teaching in a secondary modern school. He then lectured at a university in U.K.; he eventually came to Makerere in 1962 where he was recently made Professor of English. He has been concerned with scholarly editions of *Volpone*, *The Country Wife* and Elizabethan/Jacobean dramatic documents; and has published critical writings on seventeenth-century and modern drama.